A Guide
to
Santiago Cathedral

Alejandro Barral Iglesias
Ramón Yzquierdo Perrín

Edilesa

A Guide
to
Santiago Cathedral

Editor in Chief: Vicente Pastor

Layout: V. Pastor and J. Alegre
Photomechanics: Base 5
Photocomposition and Infography: LetterMAC
Printed by: Eujoa

Translated from Spanish by: Gordon Keitch

Photos: Norberto
        Publisher's Archives (20, 22 and 26b)
        Pío García (51, 68, 69, 102 and 138)

© *Text:* Alejandro Barral Iglesias
        Ramón Yzquierdo Perrín

© EDILESA
  General Sanjurjo, 7, 24001-LEON, Spain.
  Tel (987) 22 10 66

I.S.B.N.: 84-8012-066-5
Depósito Legal: AS-1.069-1994
Printed in Spain / Impreso en España

Contents

Preceding page: *Obradoiro Face, detail of the top. St James the Pilgrim at the Holy Door.*

The Building
in
History

When in the first years of the 9th Century, Bishop Theudemirus discovered St James the Apostle's remains, nobody could imagine that the cult of such venerable relics would bring about a continual flow of people who would render prophetic the words of the Calixtine Codex: *"all peoples will make pilgrimage until the end of the centuries"*.

The Goodyear Reredos. Detail of the Moving of the Apostle.

THE DISCOVERY OF THE SEPULCHRE
THE MAUSOLEUM, FROM ITS ORIGINS TO THE PRESENT

T*HE OLD TRADITION*, which goes back to the beginning of Christianity, includes the memory of the preaching and burial of St James the Great in Hispania, and in its western regions, at *Finis Terrae*, overlooking the Sea of the Britons. This is remembered in the 7th Century by St Aldhelm, Bishop of Malmesbury in England, in a poem dedicated to the Apostle: "As a first fruit of the Gospel, St James converted the Hispanic peoples with his preaching."

The same tradition -the places where he preached and the location of his Tomb- is present in the Germanic Spain of the 5th-7th Centuries and is recorded in the writings of St Isidore of Sevile. The burial place is given as *Arca Marmárica*.

After the Moorish invasion of 711 and the destruction of the Visigothic Kingdom of Toledo, the emerging Astur-Galician state kept the tradition alive. The hymn *Oh Dei Verbum*, composed in the time of King Mauregato (783-788) acclaims the evangelizing apostle and patron of Christian Spain.

The universal tradition is echoed by the *Compostelan local setting*, embodied in *Pope Leo's Letter*. It is the oldest known document, the extant version being an 11th Century one, although the data in it sets the original at the end of the 5th-Century or beginning of the 6th. The Letter contains information about the *Removal by sea* of the Holy Body, from Palestine to Iria Flavia after martyrdom by beheading at the hands of King Herod (Acts 12,2) and of its burial at *Arcas Marmáricas* (sub Arcis Marmáricis) in the western city, twelve miles from Iria. The name of the city is not given, but the topics mentioned are charged with local colour and related with the Tomb: Iria, referred to as *Bisria*, from the confluence of two rivers, the Ulla and the Sar; and the names of the disciples Theodore and Atanasius. It is one of the first hagiographic writings about St James, and as a biography of the saint, it includes some very early memories of the Spanish Church and Galicia.

Drawings by Vega y Verdugo (mid 17th Century)

Top: Apse
Bottom: West Face

THE DISCOVERY OF ST JAMES'S TOMB IN THE 9TH CENTURY. The Discovery of the sepulchre of St James the Great at *Arcis Marmáricis* between 820 and 830 is recorded in Compostelan documents from the 9th to the 12th Centuries. At the edge of the Mahía (Amaea) in the old diocese of Iria Flavia, Pelayo the hermit and the congregation of the very old church of St Felix of *Solobio*, the parish at the *foot of the forest*, experienced a *divine revelation*: in the depth of the forest they saw *luminaries* and heard *angelical songs*. Theudemirus, the bishop of Iria Flavia, came to the forest and found the *mausoleum*, which he identified without hesitating as the Apostle's tomb.

This was the discovery, *the finding* of St James's Tomb, the place of *Sant-Iago* (=Saint James), the only one where a sepulchral cult is known. Leaving his see at Iria Flavia, Theudemirus stayed to live at Arcis. Excavations in the Cathedral subsoil have revealed his tombstone (now on display in the Museum), to confirm the medieval tales. Alfonso II the Chaste (791-842) on being informed by Theudemirus immediately came to *Arcis Marmáricis* accompanied by the royal family and the Oviedo court and, according to Hispanic tradition, placed himself in St James's care.

The chaste king lost no time in sending news of the find to Aix-la-Chapelle. The Asturian court formed part of the great cultural movement of the *Court of Charlemagne* and his successors, the Carolingian kings. This cultural movement was the first *renaissance in the West*, and was to form the basis of life in medieval Europe. Literature and the iconography of Aix and Compostela concede importance to Charlemagne's rôle in the discovery of the apostle's tomb. Behind the legend, an initiative by Aix and Carolingian scribes is to be descried in the identification of *Arca Marmárica*, in the places of the west, where documents said St James's Tomb was situated.

Miniatures from the Tumbo A.

Top: *Alfonso II* Bottom: *Discovery of St James's Tomb*

The discoverers saw *proof*, with which, in the light of the documents of Iria Flavia, of which testimony exists, they identified the Tomb, abandoned since the 7th Century. They interpreted the proof as a divine revelation of the restoration of the old sepulchre cult at the place of the luminaries, which emerged with great intensity in the first half of the 9th Century, as is testified by Floro of Lyons: "The bones of the Holy Apostle were brought to Spain and deposited at the edge of that country overlooking the British Sea to be worshipped with renowned veneration by those people".

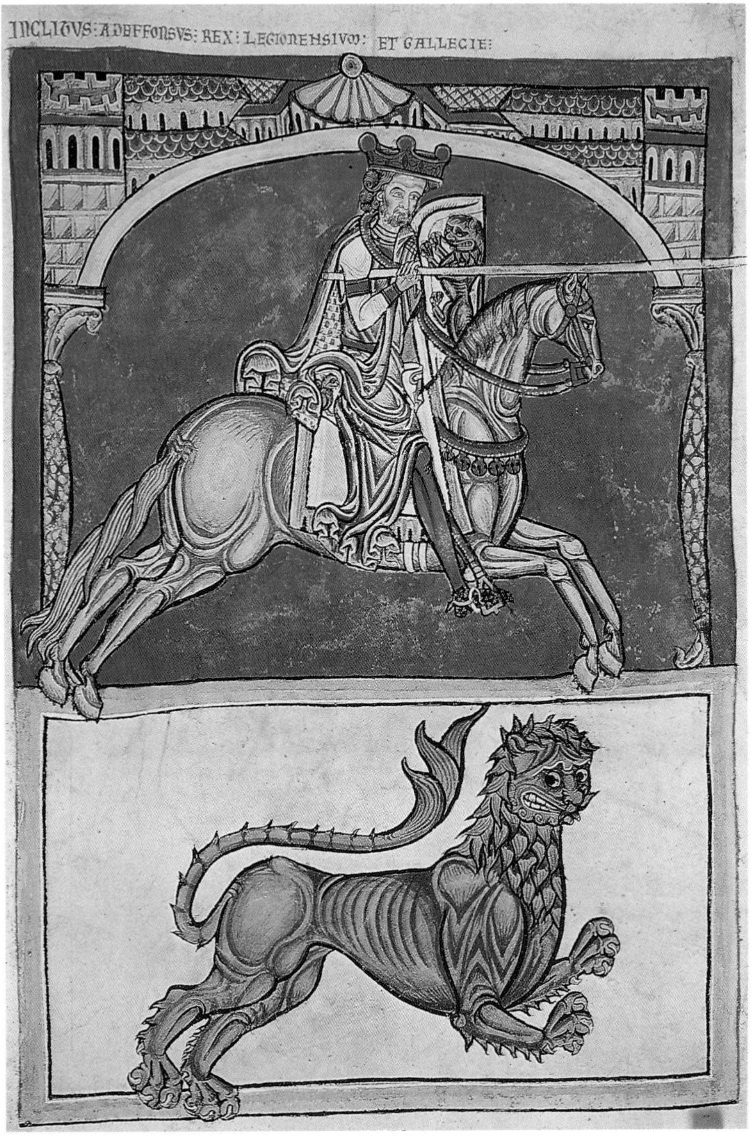
INCLITVS: ADEFFONSVS: REX: LEGIONENSIVM: ET GALLECIE:

Compostela: The Holy Place of the Apostle's Burial. The city must have come to a sudden end. A thick layer of clay covered the necropolis, where no later burials took place, a sign of its abandonment. Archeological studies of the last century broke the silence concerning the Tomb and the Apostle's sepulchre cult, and excavations around the Tomb have brought to light important historical data such as the remains of Roman constructions and the Roman and Germanic Christian necropolises in use from the 1st Century to the 7th.

The western city is identified with *Asseconia*, a Romanized Celtic city on the itinerary of Antonino. Old structures from it are still in existence and have given shape to today's Compostela. It is the Castro de la Mahía, a Roman route centre.

The mausoleum is situated in a large *pagan necropolis* (Quintana Square) to the west of the city, to which the Christian cemetery was soon to be added. It is the *place of St James*, which was known as *Arcis Marmáricis*, surely in reference to the sepulchre as the name of the place is the same as the traditional toponym. In the 10th Century another toponym emerges, that of *Compostella*, taken as "the cemetery where St James's sepulchre is". (It is also interpreted as "small well laid-out town"). The *old settlement* became a municipality in the 11th- Century, with the name Santiago de Compostela. (*Campus Stellae* is an erudite formation alluding to the luminaries at the discovery.)

The Apostle's Tomb. It was originally a late 1st Century Roman mausoleum like many others to be found all over the Empire.

Medieval documents call it the *domúncula*, or little house of the Apostle. It was made up of an upper oratory, the *cella memoriae*, from which one entered the *vaulted sepulchral chamber*: the underground crypt, known as the *parva arquata domus*. The mausoleum appears surrounded by a new structure, a corridor around the Tomb formed by a wall and dated in the middle of the 2nd Century. Worthy of especial note are the paleo-Christian 2nd- Century *second pavement* and the *Ara de Antealtares* (on show in the Museum). It was the *Title* of the mausoleum, with the inscription "dedicated to the Manes. Atia Moeta arranged in her will for this epitaph to be placed for the eternal sleep of Viria Moeta, her beloved niece aged sixteen, and provided for her own burial". Removed in the first centuries for use as the altar of the Tomb, it is very suggestive as it links traditions with legends about the saint.

Miniature from the Tumbo A: Alfonso IX, during whose reign the Romanesque Cathedral was consecrated.

CATHEDRAL OF SANTIAGO DE COMPOSTELA

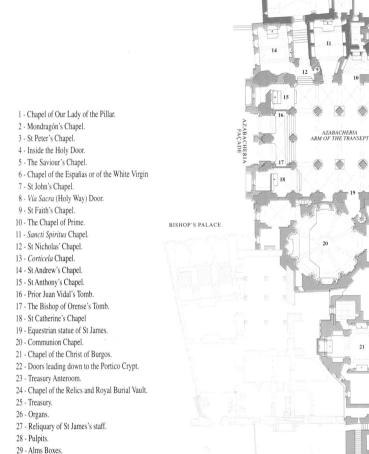

1 - Chapel of Our Lady of the Pillar.
2 - Mondragón's Chapel.
3 - St Peter's Chapel.
4 - Inside the Holy Door.
5 - The Saviour's Chapel.
6 - Chapel of the Españas or of the White Virgin
7 - St John's Chapel.
8 - *Vía Sacra* (Holy Way) Door.
9 - St Faith's Chapel.
10 - The Chapel of Prime.
11 - *Sancti Spiritus* Chapel.
12 - St Nicholas' Chapel.
13 - *Corticela* Chapel.
14 - St Andrew's Chapel.
15 - St Anthony's Chapel.
16 - Prior Juan Vidal's Tomb.
17 - The Bishop of Orense's Tomb.
18 - St Catherine's Chapel
19 - Equestrian statue of St James.
20 - Communion Chapel.
21 - Chapel of the Christ of Burgos.
22 - Doors leading down to the Portico Crypt.
23 - Treasury Anteroom.
24 - Chapel of the Relics and Royal Burial Vault.
25 - Treasury.
26 - Organs.
27 - Reliquary of St James's staff.
28 - Pulpits.
29 - Alms Boxes.
30 - Juan Beltrán de Guevara's Tomb.
31 - Doorway and access to the Royal Door of Quintana.
32 - Baptismal Font.
33 - Martín López's Tomb and the Clavijo Tympanum.
34 - Cloister Door.
35 - Sacristy Door.
36 - *Alba* (Dawn) Chapel.
37 - Chapter Library.
38 - Chapterhouse.

© *Edilesa*

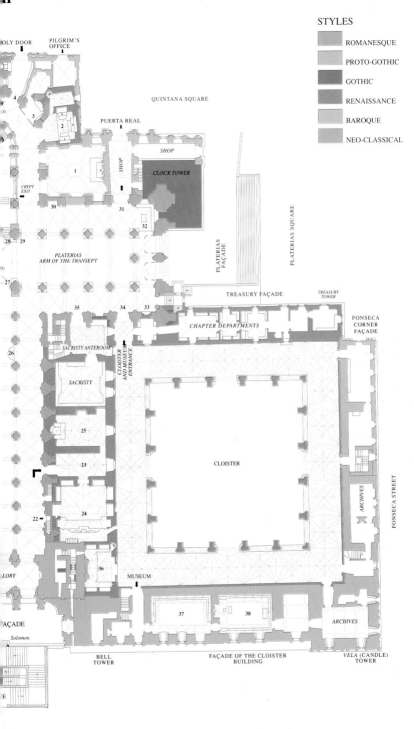

STYLES

- ROMANESQUE
- PROTO-GOTHIC
- GOTHIC
- RENAISSANCE
- BAROQUE
- NEO-CLASSICAL

HOLY DOOR

PILGRIM'S OFFICE

QUINTANA SQUARE

PUERTA REAL

4

3

2

(5)

SHOP

SHOP

CLOCK TOWER

1

CRYPT EXIT

30

31

32

28   29

PLATERIAS ARM OF THE TRANSEPT

PLATERIAS FAÇADE

PLATERIAS SQUARE

27

TREASURY FAÇADE

TREASURY TOWER

35   34   33

FONSECA CORNER FAÇADE

CHAPTER DEPARTMENTS

26

SACRISTY ANTEROOM

CLOISTER AND MUSEUM ENTRANCE

SACRISTY

25

CLOISTER

23

22

24

ARCHIVES

FONSECA STREET

36

MUSEUM

LORY

37   38

ARCHIVES

FAÇADE

Solomon

BELL TOWER

FAÇADE OF THE CLOISTER BUILDING

VELA (CANDLE) TOWER

E

UARE

The Outside
of the
Cathedral

The Cathedral is the origin and raison d'être of the city
of Santiago and the centre of its development. The old
streets lead to it, and around it are some of the most
beautiful squares bequeathed to us by the Baroque
period. The uplifting force of its towers and pinnacles
tells us nothing about the Romanesque austerity of
the inside, while hiding its real volume.

Cross of the Farrapos (Rags)

The external views of Santiago Cathedral are just as majestic as the inside, and are the product not only of its architectural volumes and the wealth and quality of sculptures, but also of the splendid squares around it. Baroque town planners knew how to create these open spaces and thus to emphasise the intrinsic values of the building by allowing for us to walk round it and see it from the most unusual angles.

According to the *Calixtine Codex*, the Cathedral had "three great porticoes and seven small ones". Only the Platerías façade and the Holy Way door are as they were in the Middle Ages, the others having been rebuilt or lost.

The first doorways were at the ends of the transept and the nave and its aisles. The subjects represented followed a plan. So the north face, also known as the *Francigena* or Paradise Façade, was dedicated to creation, sin and the promise of redemption, which was developed on the southern or Platerías doorway, which has undergone many changes down the centuries. Finally, the west door was to be given over to the transfiguration of Christ, but this was never done.

PLATERIAS SQUARE

One of the most familiar parts of Santiago, its planning started in the 16th Century and in the 18th it acquired its present nobility and monumentality. Even then it was presided over by a fountain. The present one, the Fountain of the Horses, dates from the second quarter of the 19th Century. The Cathedral borders two sides of the square.

The Platerías Façade

It stands at the southern end of the transept and is the only Romanesque face of the Cathedral. One is taken aback by its architectural organization and by the number of reliefs on its walls, which the art historian Focillon likened to a museum.

Platerías Façade

Its architecture has undergone no changes and at the very most it has been masked by the addition of reliefs or new buildings such as the Clock Tower and the Treasury. The double doorway, flanked by windows that are now hardly visible, is due to the organization of the transept. Over the archivolts there is a large frieze of reliefs and sculptures by different masters. A row of corbels of diverse decoration precedes the upper windows. Their decoration with vegetable motifs is typical of Mateo's workshop in the 13th Century. An earlier work is the figure of Mary, set between the arches, and forming an Annunciation together with the Gothic angel on the left. The façade is finished off with a Baroque balustrade.

The shafts of the doorway piers are of different materials: local marble for the outer ones and granite for the others. On the former, different sculptors have wrought apostles, saints and angels, nearly all of them delicately executed and surrounded by architectural devices. The capitals bear subjects ranging from figurative topics such as the Fall on the first one on the left, to braids and vegetable motifs. There are figures set into the jambs: Moses, St Andrew and a crossbowman in the left-hand doorway, and on the right a possible Melchizedek over an inscription of 1103 and women with animals, brought from the north face.

The tympana bear episodes from the life of Christ, the left-hand one showing His temptations. The scenes are cut on separate slabs, cut round and forced into place, which makes Duraliat think they are older than the doorways. They are attributed to the Master of the Temptation, who must also have worked at Conques. On the far right is a "masterpiece of the Master of Platerías": a seated woman whose mantle leaves one of her breasts naked while highlighting the other with its concentric folds, her legs being treated in the same way. On her lap there is a skull, which, according to the *Calixtine*, is "the rotten head of her lover, severed by her husband, who makes her kiss it twice a day". Despite such a horrifying story, the figure is interpreted today as Eve.

The same Master of the Temptation may be responsible for the Adoration of the Magi on the right-hand tympanum, although its bad condition does not allow for proof. Below it there are scenes of the Passion: the arrest, the Cyrenean with the cross, the lashes and the coronation. On the far left is the healing of the blind man. The intervention of several sculptors is evident from the differences in the reliefs, some of which, for instance that of the betrayal by Judas, are reminiscent of one of the master craftsmen active in León, who made other pieces in Santiago easy to recognize from the expressiveness of their faces and the treatment of cloth.

The diversity of subjects on the tympana, the cut-outs and the unusual disposition of some pieces have led people to consider them due to a repair following the Cathedral fire of 1117, which must have been particularly damaging to this doorway. According to Naesgaard, they must have formed part of a second programme. From the cymae, "fierce lions" guard the doors.

The frieze has been said to resemble a chaos, an impression due to alterations and additions. According to the *Calixtine*, it originally showed the apostles presided over by Christ and flanked by St Peter and St James. Of this ensemble, only four images remain on the left and five on the right, all in bad condition. The fire of 1117 occasioned an immediate repair to the west door with pieces sculpted in marble. They depict Moses and Abraham and are situated below the splendid Christ giving His blessing, a veritable *"Beau Dieu"* set in the centre of the façade and dating from around 1200. To the right is St James among trees, his inscriptions, like Abraham's, integrating him in a transfiguration, a subject chosen for the west gable end.

Other reliefs come from the Paradise, or *Francigena,* (so-called for being at the end of the "French Route" – *translator's note*) doorway, demolished in 1758. For example, the pantocrator on the left

abutment used to preside over its frieze, where it was surrounded by a tetramorph, of which the sign of St Matthew is now on the Platerías façade, before a Fall also taken from the same doorway. A little further right there is a centaur shooting an arrow, again from the Paradise doorway, probably originally forming part of a representation of the months, and with which perhaps we should connect the mermaid and fish situated a little farther away.

Although not mentioned in the *Calixtine*, the scene on the left-hand abutment, taken to be the creation of Adam, must also have belonged to the Paradise façade. Below it is the magnificent figure of David, a prefiguration of Christ triumphant and an important work of the Master of the Platerías. Opposite is the representation of Eve and farther down is Isaac's sacrifice with standing figures, executed by master craftsmen from the Platerías workshop.

Platerías Square. In the background, the Chapter House (Sarela, 1759)

The Clock Tower

Adjoining the Platerías face is an impressive tower with arches springing from it. It was built for purposes of defence at the beginning of the 14th Century, and the arches in the 15th, when the figures set into the north and east sides of the upper part of the tower were made, which are partly visible from Quintana Square.

This base was used by Domingo de Andrade for the *Clock Tower*. In the bottom tier, which is square and has slender round turrets at the corners, he set the clock faces and the main bell. For decoration he used his peculiar strings of fruit and military trophies. The second tier is octagonal and houses the chiming bell. Here the turrets and decorative devices are repeated, while the ovals over the arches bear the date 1680. Finally a balustrade surrounds the dome, which is extradosed with rich Jacobean* decoration and topped out with a lantern. Its setting, together with the harmony of its proportions and decoration make this tower a masterpiece of the Baroque period and one of the symbols of Santiago Cathedral. Andrade drew inspiration from Renaissance models, to which he was able to give new life.

The clock, which for many years has overseen life at Compostela, was made by Andrés Antelo in 1831 and commissioned by Archbishop Friar Rafael de Vélez, who paid 90,000 reales for it. The *bells* were made in 1729 by Pedro de Güemes in Santiago, and were in use until a few years ago, when they cracked, replicas being cast in Asten, Holland on the 21st December, 1989, to be hung in the tower in February, 1990. The original bells are in the cloister.

*Here and throughout this book the term Jacobean is used in reference to St James the Great.

The Treasury Façade

To the other side of the Platerías doorway stands the Treasury Façade, the west side of the cloister, which has largely defined this square, remodelled in the 18th Century. It was planned by Rodrigo Gil de Hontañón in 1540 and approved three years later. It looks like a palace and was inspired by the Monterrey Palace in Salamanca. The ground floor, used for silverware shops, which give the square its name and character (*platería*=silverware) is conceived as a base for the other two stories. The first-floor windows, crowned with pediments, are covered with grilles made in the last third of the 16th Century. The top floor is organized as a gallery. Between the windows are shields of the city, the Chapter and of Charles I, together with medallion portraits of Biblical and historical characters laid out according to a complex programme. The wall is topped out with openwork crenellation and large scrolls.

The Treasury Tower

At the southern end Rodrigo Gil built another palatial tower, at the base of

Left: Two views of the Clock Tower

Treasury Façade. East wall of the Cloister. In the foreground: the Fountain of the Horses.

which a *bronze plate*, made by Benlliure, was placed in 1915 in memory of Cardinal Martín de Herrera. The most outstanding feature of this tower is the stepped pyramid with geometrical decorations that tops it out. This finishing touch has been linked with the pre-Hispanic art of Mexico, notably with the pyramid of El Tajín. Opponents of this idea consider it to be connected with Italian treatises on architecture. At the southeast corner of the cloister, in the 17th-Century, Jácome Fernández built the *Torre de la Vela* (Candle Tower), which he modelled on the Treasury Tower.

The *Shell* of the Treasury

An access to the *Treasury Room* from the transept was built in 1705

under the direction of Simón Rodríguez. It was built to resemble the Renaissance façade and a shell-shaped projection decorated with St James's cross houses the stairway, resembling the squinches in the Chapel of Our Lady of the Pillar, designed by Andrade.

The Façade of Fonseca Corner

The building of a structure backing onto the south side of the cloister, between this and the Treasury Tower, brought about the formation of the *Fonseca Corner*, where in 1720 Fernando de Casas built a narrow façade only one fifth as wide as it is high, the design incorporating recesses and projections.

THE EAST END OF THE CATHEDRAL

The *Chevet of the Cathedral* was made up of chapels and doorways which gave rise to an irregular façade whose asymmetry set off the straight bare wall of the Monastery of Antealtares. The sight of it made Canon Vega y Verdugo consider it necessary to build a monumental wall round it, which, together with the flight of steps between the two buildings, and the levelling of the land, formed Quintana Square, "one of the most beautiful Baroque ensembles", according to Professor Bonet. This ambitious plan was not finished until the 18th Century, and its result is the impressive view of the Cathedral from this side, onto which the Royal, the Holy and the Abbots' doors open out.

The *Puerta Real* (Royal Door)

The *Royal Doorway* is part of Vega y Verdugo's project and, although the ori-

Left: *Treasury Tower and the Fonseca Corner Façade*

View of the East End of the Cathedral with the Holy Door.

ginal structure was partly made use of, it may be considered as the work of Domingo de Andrade, as is born out by the decoration with strings of fruit and military trophies. The piece crowning it was once the plinth of an equestrian statue of St James, and bears the date 1700. Walking into the transept of the Cathedral where St John the Baptist's Chapel used to stand, one is immediately struck by the vaults, from which hang stone screens bearing St James's crosses.

At the foot of the Clock Tower and beside the Royal Door is the façade of the old *Guardhouse*. Gigantic columns and pilasters on a high base frame windows with the armorial bearings of the Chapter and Archbishops Carrillo and Monroy on the first storey, while the upper ones are crowned with scrolls. On the other side of the doorway, the back wall of the Chapel of Our Lady of the Pillar has similar windows.

The Pilgrim's Office

A simple door leads to the office where there once stood a chapel where pilgrims used to receive Communion and where they now receive *the Compostela*, or certificate of pilgrimage, provided that they have made the journey on foot, by bicycle or on horseback, and for religious reasons. This credential, as in the past, gives the bearer certain rights.

Left: *Royal Door.*

Pilgrim's Office.

The *Puerta Santa* (Holy Door)

The Holy Door was built at the beginning of the 17th Century, when a doorway was made that years later was to be widened and decorated with more images of Old Testament characters and Apostles from the demolished stone choir, made by Master Mateo and his workshop. Andrade intervened in the crowning of the façade. The figures of St James and his two disciples are by Pedro del Campo, who finished them in 1694. This door is kept closed except in Holy Compostelan (Jubilee) Years, years when St James's Day (25th July) falls on a Sunday.

At the sides of the passage inside leading to the ambulatory are the walls of the Romanesque chapels of the Saviour, on the right, and of St Peter, the bare wall on the left.

Holy Doorway

Top: *General view*

Right: *Detail of figures taken from the Stone Choir.*

Following double page: *Two Prophets from the Holy Doorway: Daniel* (left) *and Isaiah* (right).

The *Puerta de los Abades* (Abbots' Door), or *Corticela* Door

At the top of the steps leading up from Quintana Square is the *Abbots' Door, or Corticela Door*, built in 1662, above which Archbishop Carrillo's shield is to be noticed. The rest of the doorway is sober, even classicist, as is brought out by the bolster work, salients and ornamental balls above.

The wall, on which Peña de Toro worked, is topped out by a balustrade with graceful pinnacles ending in balls, full of classical echoes. These are seen again on the walls of the ambulatory and the chancel, where they are distinctive. This Baroquization also affected the top of the Gothic *tambour* in 1669: once more, Vega y Verdugo's plan was adhered to, again with the balustrade with its pinnacles, an austere dome being built which covered and respected the Gothic vault. The lantern was remodelled by Andrade around 1700.

In the northeast corner the grading and simplicity of the architectural volumes of the *Corticela* stand out. Today the eaves seem very low as the neighbouring street level has risen. Next to it is the *door to St Andrew's Chapel*, emblazoned with a great shield of Archbishop Girón, commissioned in 1673 from Miguel de Erbay.

Abbots' or Corticela Doorway

Right: *Azabachería Façade*

THE AZABACHERIA FAÇADE

The *Azabachería Façade* replaced the *Francígena*, Paradise or northern Doorway described in the *Calixtine Codex*, demolished because of its ruinous state in 1758.

The square is the fruit of the agreement reached at the end of the 17th Century between the Chapter and the monks of St Martin Pinario "for the disencumbering and beautifying of the entrances ...to the Cathedral and Monastery", whose outer walls were built in the 18th Century, and those of the adjoining Bishop's Palace, in the mid 19th. Opposite were the underground money changers' offices.

The Azabachería Façade was designed by Lucas Caaveiro,who was assisted in the building by Clemente Sarela. The change from Baroque to neo-Classical in 1765 and the suggestions of Ventura Rodríguez to adjust its finishing to the dispositions of the Royal Academy caused his disciple Domingo Lois Monteagudo to finish the piece in 1769.

The doorways still follow the Compostelan Baroque formulae of the 18th Century, but a compromise solution is sought in the pediments of the side windows allowing for a neo-Classical air in the second storey. In the centre stands the image of Faith, for which Gambino was paid in 1764, and which still has a Rococo air. The façade is topped out with pediments and military trophies at the sides, with an attic supported by atlantes in the centre, atop which stands St James as a pilgrim flanked by the kneeling figures of Alfonso III and Ordoño II. These figures, and the medallions over the central windows are by Máximo Salazar, who was active in Santiago from 1766 to 1768.

OBRADOIRO SQUARE

Through the covered passage of *Gelmírez's Palace*, we come to the most splendid of Santiago's squares, and one of the most beautiful in Spain: *Obradoiro Square*, which has been since the Baroque period the main scene of city pageantry.

The Obradoiro Façade

From the square one enters the Cathedral up a monumental *flight of steps* built in the Renaissance style at the beginning of the 17th Century by Ginés Martínez. For Vega y Verdugo it is "so strange in its arrangement and architecture that nobody fails to admire its beauty". It leads up to the loggia, which runs like a magnificent balcony along the *Obradoiro Façade*. The grilles were commissioned in 1791 from Antonio García, who may have followed a plan by Lucas Ferro Caaveiro, who took charge of the Obradoiro on the death of Fernando de Casas in 1749.

The Portico of Glory had a façade which is known from documents, from drawings by Vega y Verdugo and from remains. The medieval gable end was altered as from the first years of the 16th Century, work continuing until the mid 18th Century. From it came the figures of *David and Solomon*, now on the balustrade of the loggia, though their backs were resculpted and Solomon was given a new head.

Knowledge of the structure of the medieval façade permitted Casas to demolish it as from 1738 without damaging the vaults or the construction of

Obradoiro Façade.

Preceding double page: *Night view of the Cathedral from the Herradura.*

the old *mirror* (rose window so-called became it reflected the setting sun –*translator's note*) or the splendid doorway. He conceived the central part as a spectacular Jacobean reredos presided over by the image of St James as a pilgrim, revered by Hispanic monarchs, standing in an upper niche. Below him is a representation of the amazing finding of the urn containing his remains, flanked by his disciples Anastasius and Theodore. At the bases of the towers are the images of Zebedee and St Salome, St James's parents, while on the buttresses are the effigies of St Susan and St John, on the northern tower, and St James Alphaeus and St Barbara on the southern one. They were made around 1746-48 by such local sculptors as Gregorio Fernández, José Gambino, Antonio López, Francisco Lens and Antonio Nogueira. The shafts of the columns are thoroughly worked, and on the doorways, besides the royal arms and those of the archbishop and chapter, there is an abundance of Jacobean symbols and other ornamentation.

The bronzes adorning the hinges of the doors were made in Córdoba by Esteban de Villanueva in 1609 and 1610. The nails studding the leaves of the doors were cast by Nicolás and Manuel Vidal in 1772.

The Bell Tower

The designer of the Obradoiro steps, Ginés Martínez, also built a buttress for the *Bell Tower*, which also required later work, which made it easy for Peña de Toro to carry out Vega y Verdugo's wishes and alter it in the mid 17th Century. He added pilasters to the upper-

most tier of the medieval tower and then built a new storey on top for the bells, one of the shields there being engraved with the date 1668. This phase was finished in 1671 with the placing of the cross and the weather vane on the belfry.

After 1720, there are records of further work on the tower in reference to a new topping out. Slow progress and the fact that the tower was struck by lightning in 1729 caused work to go on until 1732. The builder of the last two tiers was Fernando de Casas, who used an abundant and voluminous decoration easily visible from the square and surroundings.

The *Torre de la Carraca* (Rattle Tower)

At the same time as the decision was made to construct the Obradoiro doorway, it was also agreed to build the *Rattle Tower*, the twin of the Bell Tower, on which it is modelled and which completes the façade of the Cathedral. It takes its name from the rattle once housed in it and used in Holy Week, remains of it still existing. Building was under way in 1749 and was over in 1751.

Of such a splendid frontispiece one could say what Vega y Verdugo said of the medieval façade that preceded it: "it is one of the best that Spain has", and its praises have been sung by contemporary poets like Gerardo Diego:

For stone as well, if there are stars, will fly.
Away over the bevelled and frigid night
Grow and ascend, oh twin lilies of daring
/height;
Grow, towers, into the Compostelan sky.

Top: *Solomon and David on the Obradoiro Steps*

Bottom: *In the Portico Crypt, keystones with angels bearing the sun and moon.*

The cost of so much wonder, according to López Ferreiro, "barely exceeded forty thousand duros".

The Crypt of the Portico of Glory

The difference in the lie of the land between the Cathedral and Obradoiro Square, which made it necessary to build a monumental flight of steps, is sufficient to house a crypt, often called the "old Cathedral", access to which is available through a door situated in the centre of the lower part of the steps. Some people had thought the beginning of the crypt to predate Master Mateo, but today nobody doubts that he built it and that Burgundian influence was present. The main purpose of the crypt is to support the Portico of Glory.

Opposite the entrance is a slender Gothic figure of St James Alphaeus. In the depth of a simple porch, its sides affected by the building of the Obradoiro steps, is the double doorway, richly decorated with ornate sculpting.

Through it one reaches a sort of transept with novel ribbed vaults with angels on their bosses, one holding the sun and the other a crescent moon. Their particularities reveal them to be the work of two different craftsmen. For Professor Moralejo, these angels complete the message of the Portico of Glory, as they show that this part represents the Earth, which needs the heavenly bodies to give it light, while above, the New Jerusalem of the Apocalypse "needed neither sun nor moon...for it was lit by the glory of God". At the ends there are simple doors, only the north one in use today, which lead up to the nave and its aisles. According to some

authors, this was the only link between the crypt and the basilica until the beginning of the 17th Century.

A thick central pillar with eight piers holds up the arches of the vaults of the ambulatory formed around it, and the ribs of the barrel vaults. At the centre of this quite unusual ambulatory there is a rectangular chapel on the back wall of which slender piers support pointed arches flanking a round one, an organization used in other parts of the Cathedral. At either side there are two niches, the first semicircular and the other rectangular.

Three of these niches frame fragments of sculptures, considered by some to come from the west door described in the *Calixtine*, and by others to be from the hypothetical façade of the crypt itself. Especially noteworthy are the folds of their garments carved so as to look wet, a technique seen elsewhere, for example on the keystone showing an angel with a crescent moon. They could have formed part of the crypt, although their maker's work is not like Master Mateo's, despite their being contemporaries, the pieces being dated 1170-1175.

The capitals show a variety of types and treatment. Most follow Burgundian models and some are by Mateo. The activity of a workshop other than Mateo's must have been short-lived.

The Cloister Building and the *Torre de la Vela* ("Candle Tower")

To the right of the Obradoiro stands the wall of the cloister building, designed by Juan de Herrera –no relation to the architect of the same name who built El Escorial– and Gaspar de Arce, in the last quarter of the 16th Century. In 1614 Jácome Fernández added the upper gallery to it, bearing in mind the view from the streets and squares when he designed the corbels. If the columns with abaci supporting the lintels recall 16th-Century solutions, the same is true of Jácome Fernández's 17th-Century *Torre de la Vela*, inspired by the Treasury Tower. Lucas Caaveiro's rebuilding after the 1751 fire, which affected the inner rooms is the cause of the Baroque decorations on the balcony windows. The iron balustrades of the balcony were made by Pedro del Canto in the first years of the 17th Century, and were used as a pattern for the window grilles, to which decorative strips were added.

Left: *Crypt of the Portico of Glory.*

Detail of the west face of the Cloister and the Candle Tower.

The Inside
of the
Cathedral

«In this church there is no crack or imperfection, it is
magnificently built, it is large, spacious, bright,
harmonious, well proportioned in width, length and
height, and of admirable and inexpressibly wonderful
construction. Whoever goes up and walks the aisles of
the triforium, even if he goes up sad, will soon become
content and joyful on beholding the splendid
beauty of the church.».
(Calixtine Codex, Book V, Chapter 9)

General view of the Nave.

THE MAUSOLEUM TODAY

The historical vicissitudes of the mausoleum over twot housand years have given rise to far-reaching alterations to *St James's Tomb*.

Side doors opening off the ambulatory lead to the basement of the chancel. The present state of the mausoleum dates from the excavation made by the historian and archæologist Antonio López Ferreiro in 1878-79. What remains of it is the *plinth* and the first three courses of the *sepulchral edicule*. It was converted into an oratory with delicate architecture at the end of the 19th Century, when important Roman structures were laid bare.

In the middle is the edicule, flanked by two recesses,the mausoleum visible through its gates. It is of the Republican period, while the wall and the passage are 2nd Century. Both structures are of the classical header/stretcher arrangement.

The central door allows us to see a first chamber. To its sides are Roman bricked-up niches. Their walls are pierced with small windows: the devotional *fenestellas* of the disciples, the martyrs *Theodore and Atanasius*.

Another wall separates it from the *second chamber: the burial vault of the Holy Body*. Today, three arches on columns, which support the vaults, house a marble-fronted altar with a palæo-Christian flavour holding the *silver casket*, made by *Rey and Martínez* from drawings by *José Losada* in 1886. Inspired by the little altarpiece of Gelmírez's day, its front shows the apostles under an arcade accompanying Christ in Majesty, an imitation of the stone piece of around 1100 on show in the Museum. Inside it, a compartmented cedarwood box contains the Holy Body of Sant-Iago (=St James, whence Santiago, *translator's note*) and the remains of his two disciples. Above the urn is a symbolic star, showing the place of the Tomb.

This is the *Locus Sancti Iacobi*, centre of the age-old pilgrimage, and reason for the existence of the basilica and the Compostelan city. In the coming and going of pilgrims to the Tomb, Europe has been made. It still holds a fascinating attraction. Around the Tomb, according to the *Calixtine Codex*, pilgrims would spend the night in vigil holding lights so that the night was as bright as the day, while they intoned hymns like the *Canto de Ultreya*.

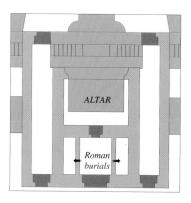

Apostle's Crypt

Top: *Passage with burials at the sides.*

Bottom: *Urn.*

PRE-ROMANESQUE CONSTRUCTIONS

When the apostle's sepulchre was discovered by Bishop Theudemirus of Iria at an uncertain date at the beginning of the 9th Century, King Alfonso II ordered the construction of a church which would respect the Roman mausoleum and facilitate the cult of the relics. He donated land to it and founded the Monastery of Antealtares.

The first thing to do was to put the mausoleum itself in order, as it was overgrown and neglected. The church built by Alfonso II, according to the consecration document in Alfonso III's basilica, was small and of stone and mud. It stood over part of a westward-facing necropolis discovered from 1946 onwards, when excavations took place in the nave and aisles of the Cathedral.

The oldest tombs go back to the Hispano-Roman period, others are 6th Century, some have roof-shaped lids with decorated arrises and the most recent ones are 11th Century. Close to the end of the nave the base was found of a turret of the defensive wall built around 900 by Bishop Sisnando and completed by his successor Cresconio in the mid 11th Century.

Something is known of Alfonso II's church, which had a nave with wooden roofing, and where the Roman sepulchre was kept in the chancel, as over it, in Alfonso III's day, a basilica was built, and consecrated in 899 before the monarch, his family, nobles, bishops and other personages.

This second church was splendidly decorated with marbles brought from a recently reconquered city, which gave them special value as an offering to the saint who was protector of the Hispanic peoples. The building was unusually proportioned and had architectural solutions of its own, in part because respecting the apostle's edicule meant building a nave almost as wide as that of the Romanesque Cathedral, and twice as wide as the aisles, from which it was separated by pillars supporting arches. On these and on the end walls rested the beams of the roof, buttresses thus being rendered unnecessary. A portico was set before the west door, and onto the north wall backed St John the Baptist's Chapel-cum-Baptistry.

Greater problems concern the setting of the three altars, other than St James's, mentioned in the document of consecration, as no trace has been found of them. Some authors say they were in the neighbouring church of the Monastery of Antealtares, where the same dedications were repeated - the Saviour, St Peter and St John the Evangelist.

The floor was made of reddish mortar with pieces of brick and quartz. Part of it remains in place and fragments are also to be seen in the *Cathedral Museum*, where other pieces from the basilica are also on show.

The importance of the cult of St James became so great that in the summer of 997 Almanzor raided Santiago, razing the city to the ground, burning churches, monasteries and palaces, according to the expressively worded

Crónica Silense. The rebuilding of the shrine by St Peter of Mezonzo, then Bishop of Compostela, and by King Bermudo II was immediate. This church welcomed pilgrims until it was demolished in 1112 to make way for the continuing building of the Romanesque Cathedral.

Top: *Theudemirus' Tombstone (d. 20th October, 847)*

Bottom: *Remains of the 9th-Century city wall and graves, under the nave.*

THE ROMANESQUE CATHEDRAL

In 1075, the progressive boom in pilgrimages to Compostela and the rites of veneration of the relics induced Bishop Diego Peláez, with King Alfonso VI's sponsorship, to begin the construction of the Romanesque Cathedral. The architectural scheme of this temple of relics is of the "pilgrimage church" type, with a symbolic Latin Cross groundplan and a wide ambulatory around the chancel permitting pilgrims to hold services in the chapels off it. The galleries overlooking the nave built over the aisles were also used as places of welcome. This pattern was repeated in other churches on the roads leading from France to Compostela: St Martial's at Limoges and St Martin's at Tours - both destroyed - St Faith's Church at Conques and St Saturninus' at Toulouse are closely linked with Santiago Cathedral, more so than with Conques Cathedral.

Construction is recorded in the *Calixtine Codex* as having begun in 1078, although an inscription in the Saviour's Chapel gives the date as 1075, adding: "The master stonemasons who began the construction of the Cathedral of Santiago are called Bernardo the Elder, an admirable master craftsman, and Roberto, with about fifty other masons working there assiduously". In 1077, the prelate came to an agreement with the abbot of Antealtares, St Fagildo, as the work affected his church. In 1088, when work was going on smoothly, Bishop Diego Peláez was deposed and imprisoned by the king on a charge of treason. The three central chapels of the ambulatory, the corresponding sections of the

wall and the enclosing of the chancel were left unfinished.

The situation arising in Santiago out of the king's drastic action could not be put right easily, so in 1092 he bestowed the title of Count of Galicia on his son-in-law, Raymond of Burgundy, who the following year chose Canon Diego Gelmírez as vicar and administrator of the diocese, of which he was consecrated Bishop in 1100. Building was recommenced, the unfinished parts were finished and the project was updated. Direction of the new workshop is usually attributed to Master Esteban, but his presence in 1101 in Pamplona Cathedral leads some to speak more in terms of one of the masters of the Platerías, as this seems to be one of the most notable parts of their work.

In this second stage the ambulatory was completed and the monumental transept was built, with four chapels in its west wall, and the north and south façades with their iconographic themes. Work was also started on the reliefs that were to be developed on the western gable end, which would close off the nave and aisles then being worked on. The rhythm of work permitted Gelmírez to consecrate some altars in 1105.

In 1112 the pre-Romanesque church was demolished and in 1117 the Cathedral was set on fire by local citizens who had risen against Gelmírez and Doña Urraca, causing extensive damage. Building continued throughout the 12th Century and, although the Calixtine

The admonishing of Adam and Eve.

Codex records it as going on for forty-four years, this is far from the truth, as the building of the nave and aisles was slow and laborious, owing both to the lie of the land and perhaps to the presence of the defences and turrets which were in the way and not taken down until 1120.

The final impulse was given in 1168 by Master Mateo, who received a pension of two silver marks a week, or a hundred morabentinos a year, from King Ferdinand II to finish building the Cathedral. He had to begin by finishing the nave and aisles and by solving the problem of the lie of the land, which he did by building a crypt, which was to become the plinth of the Portico of Glory, above which he built a gallery which was higher than the others. He

also built the façade with its two towers. At the same time as he was working on this immense project, he built the stone choir, which occupied the first sections of the nave until the 17th Century. Santiago Cathedral was solemnly consecrated in the presence of King Alfonso IX in 1211.

Since then, the construction has undergone several alterations. At the end of the Middle Ages a cloister was built, to be later demolished, and a Gothic apse was started, which, if it had been finished, would have meant the disappearance of the Romanesque building and would have made the laying out of Quintana Square impossible. Still remaining now are the sculptures presiding the High Altar, the tambour and some chapels.

The Renaissance left behind the magnificent cloister, on which some of Spain's best architects worked, altars, the bronze pulpits and Arfe's tabernacle. The age of greatest change, however, was the Baroque period, when such splendid ensembles as the Chapel of Our Lady of the Pillar, the Clock Tower, the Chancel, the *Puerta Santa*, the organs and the inimitable Obradoiro façade were built. It was also then when the wide and beautiful squares were laid out to frame the Cathedral and confer on it a special relevance to the city.

The neo-Classical period brought with it a decline parallelled by that in pilgrimages which had set in with Luther's Reformation. In spite of everything, in the 18th Century, work went on which followed Royal Academy rules in a rather peculiar manner, as is born out by the finishing of the Azabachería Door and the Chapel of the Communion.

The upheavals of the 19th Century made it a bad period for the Cathedral, when in 1879 the remains hidden in 1589 for fear of Drake were found. Santiago went through a period of deep crisis from which it did not recover until well into the 20th Century. Since the nineteen forties, remodelling and restoration work has been undertaken and Santiago Cathedral is now one of Europe's most splendid buildings, its creation being in large part due to the Pilgrims' Way.

Left: *Back wall of the Portico of Glory Crypt.*

Horses from the Royal Procession, from Master Mateo's stone choir. Column from the demolished north face.

THE AMBULATORY

Although the construction of the Cathedral began with the central chapels of the Ambulatory, it is better to see each one as we come to it in order not to have to go backwards and forwards.

Chapel of Our Lady of the Pillar(1)

It occupies the site of St Andrew's (the other side of the ambulatory from St Faith's Chapel) and St Martin's - or St Fructuoso's - the advowson of the parish it took over, and the space between the two.

In 1696, the Chapter commissioned a new sacristy from Domingo de Andrade, who directed the project until 1711, when for reasons of ill-health and age he resigned in favour of Fernando de Casas. In 1713, Archbishop Friar Antonio de Monroy had the unfinished sacristy made into the Chapel of the Virgin of the Pillar, paying the bills himself. On his death in 1715 it was still unfinished, building lasting until 1719 and decoration until 1723.

It has two entrances from the Ambulatory, a rectangular groundplan and a gigantic order of pilasters, between which there are niches for drawers, windows and diverse ornamental motifs. The dome, atop squinches crowned with enormous scallop shells bearing St James's Cross, is octagonal and decorated with shields, Jacobean motifs and vegetables expertly carved from granite. It is finished off with a lantern, also eight-sided. The ensemble of the chapel, according to Torres Balbes "the first frankly Baroque piece in Galicia", has a great wealth of decoration and of materials, with a generous use of marbles and jaspers, painted in part and badly in need of restoration.

The reredos, designed by Fernando de Casas, seems to be inspired by ephemeral constructions in Seville designed to celebrate the canonization of St Ferdinand, and gives a foretaste of architectural solutions that Casas himself was to use on the Obradoiro Façade. There are also allusions to the Basilica of the Pillar in Zaragoza. The execution of such a singular project in marbles and jaspers, inaugurated on the 12th October, 1721, was the work of Miguel de Romay. The images, except that of the chapel's namesake, are by Fernández Sande. The central niche houses the Virgin of the Pillar, brought from Zaragoza, with St James the Pilgrim prostrate before her. On the arch over the niche there is a design of leaves, heads of angels and an inscription. Higher up, a picture painted

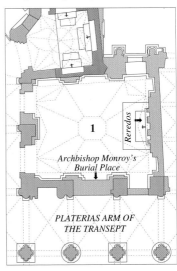

1

Reredos

Archbishop Monroy's Burial Place

PLATERIAS ARM OF THE TRANSEPT

Reredos from the Chapel of Our Lady of the Pillar.

by Antonio García de Bouzas in about 1722 represents the apparition of the Virgin to the Apostle. The reredos is topped out with a graceful Baroque dome.

The rest of the pictorial decoration of the chapel was commissioned by García de Bouzas, who thoroughly specified every detail.

Archbishop Monroy's funerary monument is covered with a large slab of black marble with an epitaph praising him. Above it a niche houses a prie-dieu with an image of the prelate kneeling and praying at it against the background of a window. It was sculpted by Fernández Sande and one's attention is caught by its realism and the pomposity of the vestments. The scene is framed by columns supporting an entablature on the cornice of which stand graceful pinnacles and the Archbishop's shield. There are also plaques typical of the Compostelan Baroque of the 17th Century.

Near the altar are some chests of drawers in mahogany and ebony with ivory and tortoiseshell inlays. They are among the most sumptuous pieces of furniture the Cathedral possesses and are contemporary with the completion of the chapel.

The doors are protected by novel bronze grilles cast in 1721 and perhaps designed by Fernando de Casas. Their uprights are the evolution of those used at the beginning of the 17th Century, and they become radial in the upper semi-circle. They also have a curious lock.

Interior of the octagonal dome with Jacobean and heraldic decoration.

Mondragón's Chapel (2)

Founded around 1521 by Canon Juan de Mondragón, this chapel has an almost rectangular groundplan under a beautiful ribbed vault. Over the sacristy a small gallery opens onto the chapel under a segmental arch. The architecture, by *Jácome García*, follows patterns and solutions used by Juan de Alava in the cloisters. To one side of the window, with its round arch, there is a shield.

Against the back wall, also under a segmental arch, is a magnificent terracotta reredos made by *Miguel Perrín* in Seville, and commissioned in 1526. It is worked very thoroughly and with great virtuosity, and retains a Gothic aftertaste. Its subject is the weeping for Christ's death, with His rigid corpse in the foreground. Before Him His mother kneels, her hands together in an attitude of extreme pain, which is shared by the apostles, disciples and holy women standing around Him. The background is a somewhat peculiar view of Jerusalem.

In 1751 an altarpiece was put up beside it with fine images of St John the Baptist, St Anthony and the monumental ones of Christ on the Cross and the Mother of Sorrows. The chapel and the altarpiece were restored and repainted in the 1830s with funding by the Marquis of Santa Cruz de Rivadulla.

Its grille is attributed to *Juan Francés*, but was probably made by one of his disciples and, although made in 1522, it follows a 15th Century pattern, but with Renaissance motifs.

Weeping for Christ's Death. Terra-cotta by Miguel Perrin.

St Peter's Chapel (3)

This chapel, which has preserved its medieval construction intact, stands beside the Holy Door. It has a fine Baroque reredos designed by *Fernando de Casas* and carved in 1731. In the centre of the main tier is Our Lady of the Lily, whose protection is sometimes attributed to this chapel. The other images: St Joseph, St Peter and (in the upper tier) St Jude Thaddeus are also of interest.

On the right is the tomb of Doña Mencía de Andrade, who endowed the chapel in 1571. The making of the granite sepulchre was commissioned by the lady herself from *Juan Bautista Celma* in 1582. Her effigy lies on its left side, with the head, covered by a mantle, resting on two pillows, which she holds with one hand in a gesture of pleasurable sleep. The right arm is held stretched along the side with a rosary in the hand. At her feet a greyhound eyes his mistress attentively. The figure, the heir to medieval prototypes is, according to Professor Rosende, "one of the most beautiful images of Galician funerary sculpture".

The vault and walls of the chapel were decorated with ornamental paintings and with an Assumption of the Blessed Virgin, today in very bad condition. They date from about 1800.

The screen, also paid for by Doña Mencía, was commissioned from *Sadornín Fernández* in 1571, and follows the pattern of the one in the Chapel of the Saviour. In general a well-made piece, the embossing on the lock is of especially good craftsmanship.

Baroque reredos. Details of St Joseph (top) and St Peter (bottom)

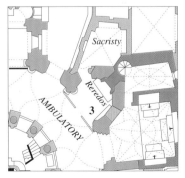

Inside the Holy Door (4)

To the right of the Saviour's Chapel, the Holy Door was built in the 16th Century, the only noteworthy pieces inside it being the figures at its sides. They were taken from the façades of the stone choir, which until the beginning of the 17th Century stood in the nave. The choir was the work of Master Mateo and his workshop, and several pieces and fragments are extant, which have permitted the reconstruction of three chairs and the reproduction of the ensemble. A consecrational cross is set on the lintel of the door.

This door is only opened during *Holy Compostelan Years* (or Jubilee Years), years in which St James's Day (25th July, *translator's note*) falls on a Sunday, which happens with intervals of five, six and eleven years. After the last one (1993), the last one of the century, and of the millennium, will be 1999.

Left: *Holy Doorway ensemble with sculptures brought from the stone choir.*

The Prophet Ezekiel (left) and St Jude (right)

Stained-glass window showing the Apostle

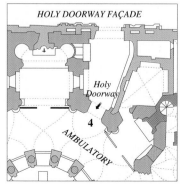

HOLY DOORWAY FAÇADE

Holy
Doorway

AMBULATORY

The Saviour's Chapel (5)

This is the central chapel of the ambulatory and the largest of the old ones, probably because of its singular semicircular back with two small alcoves. The outside, however, used to be rectangular, as may still be appreciated today and may be seen on a 17th-Century drawing.

The inscriptions born by the figures on the capitals at the entrance: *Reinando el príncipe Alfonso se construyó esta obra*, on the left, and *En tiempos del obispo Diego se comenzó esta obra*, on the right, mean respectively *This work was built during the reign of Prince Alfonso* and in the *time of Bishop Diego this work was begun.* On the side walls there remain fragments of the long inscriptions repeating these data and the work is dated 1075.

The reredos, funded by the third Archbishop Fonseca in 1532, is attributed to Juan de Alava. It is made of exquisitely worked polychromed stone. The niche in the centre of the first tier used to house the tabernacle, which in the first years of the 17th Century "always held the *Most Holy Sacrament*". Today it shelters an expressive Gothic image of the Saviour with His hands raised to show His wounds.

In this chapel, known by some people as the King of France's Chapel owing to an old foundation, foreign pilgrims could confess with priests who spoke their languages, take Communion and receive the *Compostela*, the certificate of their penitential pilgrimage.

Against the north wall is the tombstone of city treasurer Don Francisco Treviño, who died in 1511, his image on the stone holding a two-handed sword and a rosary. Buried under the floor here is the Bishop elect of Lugo and Rector of the University, Doctor Antonio Páramo y Somoza, who died in 1786. Finally, the screen, apparently Toledan, was donated by Archbishop Fonseca and made by Master Domingo.

Left: *Stone reredos in the Saviour's Chapel*

Gothic image of the Saviour.

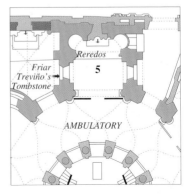

Chapel of the White Virgin, or of Our Lady of the Españas (6)

To the north –left– of the Saviour's Chapel, the White Virgin's Chapel was erected. Its foundation is attributed to Juan de España at the end of the 13th Century, but on the arch over the entrance door, at the sides of a shield, are the names of other citizens of Santiago of the last years of the 14th Century and beginning of the 15th, when the chapel was built, later to have as its patron the said Juan de España. Over the arch is one of the crosses of the consecration of the Cathedral in 1211.

Its irregular groundplan is due to its setting between the Saviour's and St John's Chapels. The ribbed vault over it is divided into four sections and its keystone is decorated with leafwork. The window on the left had a mullion until the 18th Century. Underneath it there are two arched niches, one with the founder's tomb and one 16th-Century one. Opposite is another 16th-Century

one and a fourth tomb, of the 17th Century.

The neo-Gothic reredos made by *Maximino Magariños* in 1906, with reliefs along the bottom, shows in the centre of its only storey the Baroque image of the White Virgin carved in 1744 by the Compostelan sculptor *Gregorio Fernández*. It is flanked by four figures by *Magariños*. The screen is by *Clemente Lorenzo* and its lock bears the date 1725.

Entrance and general view of the reredos.

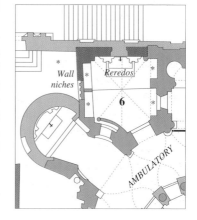

St John's Chapel (7)

This old Romanesque chapel was enlarged in the 16th and 18th Centuries when the back wall was demolished, although the vault was not touched, another, shell-shaped one being constructed during the enlargement to frame the top of the reredos. In front of it a lantern was erected and decorated with geometric plates typical of the Compostelan Baroque of the 18th Century and especially of *Simón Rodríguez*, to whom the lantern is attributed and who is buried in this chapel.

The altarpiece, also thought to be the work of this artist, shows episodes of the life of St John between its pilasters. The central part has been altered to hold the image of St Susan, co-patron of the city, carved by *Aniceto Marinas* around 1917. The saint to whom the chapel is dedicated stands in the upper niche flanked by a decoration of vegetable motifs.

The screen is also 18th-Century, and uses iron rods to form geometrical shapes. It has no stone plinth and has a curious finishing piece.

Left: *Reredos in St John's Chapel*

The old Vía Sacra *(Holy Way) Door.*

The *Vía Sacra* (Holy Way) Door (8)

Apart from the Cathedral's three main entrances, other "minor doors" were also put in, among which is the one situated between the Chapels of St John and St Faith. It was called the Vía Sacra door after the street it opened onto. It was bricked up in the 16th Century and was not reopened until 1933.

On the inside there is a lintel and no decoration. Above it there is a window with a round arch, and above that a circular window. This arrangement of lights was repeated in the sections of the ambulatory where there were no chapels and has been maintained even when chapels have been built, except over the site of St Pelayo's Door, where Mondragón's Chapel was built.

The Central Sections of the Ambulatory

Those parts of the ambulatory containing the chapels and doors already described belong to the first phase of construction. They are covered with vaults with ribless arrises, and there are no arches between the sections. Their presence, together with other details, serves to establish the beginning of the second stage. On the other side, the vaults rest on the arches and columns of the chancel, which in the 17th Century were Baroquized. On plinths of jasper and marble, solomonic columns were built to carry an entablature on which angels stood holding lamps.

The wrought-iron balusters of the intercolumns, now windows, must have been designed by Andrade in the second half of the 17th Century, and made by Compostelan smiths. The upper stained-glass windows, with gilded bronze framing and decoration, were installed by Andrés Antelo in 1818, when Múzquiz was Archbishop.

Over the ambulatory there is a gallery covered by a one-sided tunnel vault with splayed windows at its base.

The Completion of the Ambulatory

When good relations were reestablished after the expulsion of Bishop Diego Peláez, Raymond of Burgundy and Gelmírez completed what was unfinished and rounded off the ambulatory. The former is almost imperceptible on the inside but may be more clearly seen from the outside. The recommencing is easily discerned from the changes introduced: the vaults rest on arches, the working and the subjects of the capitals and mouldings are different, and greater proportions are used.

Capitals with figures in the ambulatory and transept.

Right: Northern part of the ambulatory.

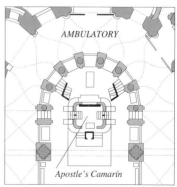

St Faith's Chapel (9)

It is traditionally said to have been erected at the beginning of the second stage of construction, after work had been completely paralysed. According to Professor Durliat, however, "work on the Cathedral was not entirely stopped... Some work was done, essentially the building and decorating of the chapels of St Faith and of St Andrew, together with the adjoining parts of the ambulatory".

The chapel is polygonal, and over a basal wall there are windows with round arches. The capitals flanking the vegetable motifs over the entrance are hagiographic. The right-hand one shows the condemning of St Faith: the executioner with his sword and her being led away for punishment. The left-hand one seems to show St Caprasio's self-accusation in the face of the former's example

on confessing her beliefs. The subjects and the dedication to St Faith are evidence of the relationship with Conques.

In 1515, Canon Gómez Rodríguez Sotomayor, who is buried in the chapel, set up a foundation and the chapel was dedicated to St Bartholomew, by whose name it is still also known. In 1521, the Cathedral schoolmaster Don Diego de Castilla, great-grandson of King Peter I, arranged in his will for his sepulchre and reredos to be commissioned from the Flemish sculptor Arnao. The reredos, because of its similarity to the one in the Saviour's Chapel, has led Professor Pita to consider it to have been made by Juan de Alava or one of his disciples. It is presided over by Our Lady of Good Counsel, flanked by St James and St Bartholomew. In the centre of the pediment is a representation of the

Christ of the Pains, antefixed by two skulls linking it with the sepulchre.

The tomb, set in the left-hand wall, is worked in soft, fine-grained lithographic stone from Coimbra, which allows for very thorough and careful workmanship. Its architectural structure is that of a triumphal arch, which does not prevent the recumbent effigy and the tomb from following medieval patterns, although the figure is notable for its realism. On the back wall of the niche, the dead man's shield is borne by chubby angels, while above is the Resurrection of Christ. On the pediment, a man shows a skull to a woman, a subject with classical overtones, as are the military trophies flanking the long and praising epitaph, and the figures topping out the pediment. It is a valuable piece of funerary art.

The screen follows the pattern of the one in the Saviour's Chapel, especially as regards the uprights. It must have been made around 1532 and is generally attributed to *Guillén de Bourse*, at the time active in Santiago, especially in the Cathedral.

Renaissance reredos (left) *and Don Diego de Castilla's Tomb* (right)

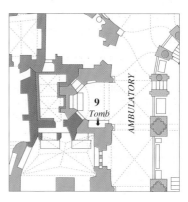

ARMS OF THE TRANSEPT

The arms of the transept, part of the second phase of the construction (1098-1122) of the Romanesque building, are the work of Master Esteban and his workshop, and were finished in 1105, when Gelmírez consecrated the altars of the chapels of the apse.

Left: General view of the transept looking south (Platerías arm)

View of the northern end (Azabachería arm) of the transept.

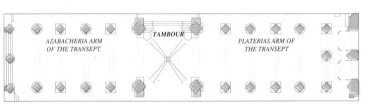

AZABACHERIA ARM OF THE TRANSEPT.

TAMBOUR

PLATERIAS ARM OF THE TRANSEPT

The Chapel of Prime (10)

The old *Brotherhood of Clergymen*, or *Choir Chaplains*, known also as the Brotherhood of the *Immaculate Conception*, already existed in the 12th Century. Their chapel is a project by *Juan de Alava*, carried out by *Jácome García* in 1523. The lack of space gave rise to the original construction with two arches, corresponding to two Romanesque sections. To the right stands a great Renaissance arch with the mausoleum of Canon Antonio Rodríguez Agustín (†1526), by *Cornielis of Holland*. It is one of the most beautiful funerary statues in Galicia. The arch on the left indicates the destroyed apsidal Chapel of the Holy Cross.

The 18th-Century reredos is the work of *Simón Rodríguez*, one of the great masters of Compostelan Baroque. In the right-hand niche stands *Our Lady of Prime*, by *Cornielis*. In the left-

hand one is a relief of the Taking Down, made by *Diego de Sande* in 1721, in memory of Gelmírez's dedication to the Holy Cross. At its feet is the burial place of Antonio Domingo de Andrade.

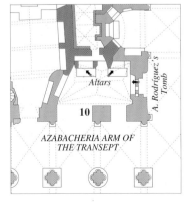

Left: *Our Lady of the Conception.*

Relief of the Taking Down from the Cross.

The *Sancti Spiritus* Chapel (11)

At the end of the Romanesque stage of construction, the citizens and clergy of Compostela began to use the spaces left by the design for chantry chapels. Such is the case of Pedro Vidal, who had a chapel built in the mid 13th Century taking up St Mary's Doorway, which gave onto the Corticela. Reformed by his great-grandson, Archdeacon Gonzalo Pérez de Moscoso, the chapel has an elongated groundplan and a pointed vault on interesting corbels. The gallery is the work of *Andrade* (1694). The doorway, built at the end of the 16th Century, has a lintel with a trifoliated arch with crenellations and towers. Above it are the wolves' heads of the Moscosos and the consecrational cross of the basilica.

There are seven tombs in the chapel. On the left is that of choirmaster Juan de Melgrejo (†1534), whose reclining effigy has an expressive face. Opposite is that of the canon Cardinal Pedro Varela (†1574).

To the left of the nave are the tombs of the merchant Francisco de la Peña, of

Archbishop Alonso Sánchez de Moscoso –with a 16th-Century mural of the Taking Down on the back wall of the niche– and of the founder, Pedro Vidal. The fronts of the sepulchres are decorated with trifoliated motifs containing thurifying angels. The artwork, as in the case of the doorway, is by Master Mateo.

To the right is the tomb of city treasurer Fructuoso Gallo (†1564) and his wife.

Against the back wall is the Baroque altar of Loneliness, dismantled and removed from the retrochoir of the Cathedral in 1945. The image of the Virgin was made in Madrid in 1666. The silver pedestal and frontal, by *Antonio Morales*, were made in 1747. The reredos is topped out with a Calvary scene, with a beautiful 14th-Century crucifix and 15th-Century figures of Mary and St John.

View of the ensemble with the reredos of Loneliness.

Right: *Archbishop Moscoso's Tomb.*

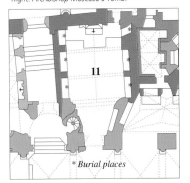

* *Burial places*

The Apsidal Chapel of St Nicholas (12)

It was the nearest chapel to the Paradise Door, by which European pilgrims used to enter, and was the foreigners' parish. It is the work of Master Esteban and was consecrated in 1105. In the 17th Century it became a thoroughfare. With its semicircular groundplan, the only one left off the transept, it retains a number of interesting architectural features: shell vault, columns, billets and windows.

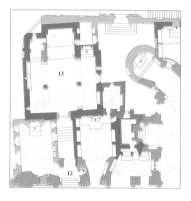

Thoroughfare to the Corticela through the Romanesque Chapel of St Nicholas.

Right: *Doorway and interior of the Corticela.*

Chapel of St Mary of the *Corticela* (13)

A corridor with a flight of steps, built in 1711, cuts across the street that used to run between the Cathedral and the monastery church of the Corticela. It was founded in the 9th Century by Alfonso II, and, owing to its limited size, gave rise to St Martin Pinario. In 1527, the *Corticela* became the parish of foreigners and Basques.

The Cathedral having been rebuilt in 1213, the *Corticela* is part of the art of Master Mateo's workshop, as is born out by the beautiful doorway with the Adoration of the Magi, which is linked with the Epiphany of Mateo's old stone choir. Its plan and elevations reflect the pattern of Alfonso III's pre-Romanesque basilica of the late 9th Century.

On the left there is a Germanic tomb with a roof-shaped lid and decorated arrises. In the arched niches are a 16th-Century Christ on the Mount of Olives and a recumbent image of the 18th Century. In the main chapel there is an image of Our Lady of Consolation, made in the 16th Century, and in the side chapel is the Christ Child of the *Teçeleiros'* (Weavers') Gild, of German origin.

On the right is the 15th-Century tomb of a lady pilgrim, the recumbent form dressed in rich Burgundian garments. The sepulchre of Cardinal Gonzalo Eáns (†1342) is an interesting example of 14th-Century sculpture.

St Andrew's Chapel (14)

Founded by Archbishop Andrés Girón in 1674, this chapel has a Baroque reredos made in 1707 by *Fernández Espantoso* and another altarpiece of Our Lady of Covadonga designed by *Simón Rodríguez* in 1733.

Against the right-hand wall are the tombs, one above the other, of Canon Pedro García (†1561) and Cardinal Juan Martínez Ternero (†1581), with reclining effigies by *Juan Bautista Celma*.

Baroque reredos of St Andrew.

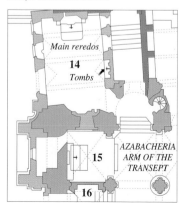

St Anthony's Chapel (15)

To the right of the platform of the Azabachería doorway, this chapel possesses an 18th-Century reredos by *Simón Rodríguez*.

Top: *St Anthony's Reredos*

Bottom: *Recumbent sculpture of Juan Vidal.*

Prior Juan Vidal's Tomb (16)

The sepulchre of Prior Juan Vidal, who died in 1582, is to the right of the Azabachería door. The highly expressive recumbent effigy is attributed to *Juan Bautista Celma.*

The Arms of the Transept and the Crossing

From the Azabachería arm, one has a view across the nave to the opposite Platerías façade along the twelve sections of the transept, totalling 65 metres. The beautiful architectural sequence is distinguished by the amplitude and slenderness of its proportions, of pondered classical rhythm and wise juxtaposition of the structural elements. The main hall and the aisles are separated by pillars backed with piers, upon which the round arches rest, their springers giving more height.

The aisles of the transept are half the height of the main hall and are enclosed by arcades and groin vaults. Over them a structural innovation is introduced: the *high gallery*, which goes round the Cathedral over the aisles and the ambulatory. It is covered by one-sided tunnel vaults and has windows overlooking the exterior and opens onto the nave and main hall of the transept via the *triforium* balconies. Its end walls have the same beautiful composition, finished off with a large rose window.

The piers backing onto the walls of the aisles break up a splendid architecture of apsidal chapels and windows, which used to flood the inside of the Cathedral with light.

Together with the perfection and beauty of its architecture goes the exquisite ornamentation of the capitals, intricately decorated with vegetable motifs, with pointed leaves and buds, or entwined around human figures.

Swinging mechanism of the Botafumeiro at the base of the Tambour.

Sepulchre of the Bishop of Orense, Alonso López de Valladolid(17)

The bishop died in 1468, and his sepulchral arch is finished off with the arms of the Mendozas. The beautiful reclining effigy is late Gothic. The bronze crozier is a fine example of precious metalwork of the time.

St Catherine's Chapel (18)

It occupies the site of what was the old Royal Burial Vault, behind the tomb of the bishop of Orense. It was funded by the Marquis and Marchioness of Bendaña. There is a late 18th Century reredos.

Reredos and image of St Catherine

Bottom: *Recumbent sculpture of the Bishop of Orense*

Right: *St James on horseback.*

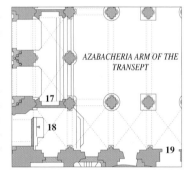

AZABACHERIA ARM OF THE TRANSEPT

17

18

19

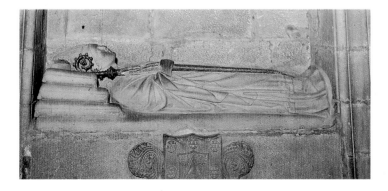

St James on Horseback (19)

A niche houses the popular equestrian figure of St James, which belongs to the Gild of Jetworkers (*Azabacheros*). It was made by the sculptor *José Gambino* in the second half of the 18th Century.

THE NAVE

Without losing the grandiosity of Romanesque architecture, it acquires the flavour of a great hall. From it one can contemplate the harmonious and bare interior of the Portico of Glory, in all its stark monumentality.

At the feet of the *Santo dos Croques* (*Headbanging Saint*, his wisdom being transmitted to those who bang their heads against his, *translator's note*), is the monumental bronze of the tomb of Archbishop Pedro Muñiz, who consecrated the Cathedral in 1211.

In the third section, a bronze trap door leads down to the excavations of the Roman and Germanic necropolises of the 1st and 7th Centuries and of Alfonso III's basilica.

The splendid rock crystal lamp was made in Germany and was used at the Great Exhibition in Paris in 1855. The Senate Lamp was donated by the Compostelan senator Eugenio Montero Ríos.

North Aisle of the Nave (bottom) *and Nave* (right).

The Communion Chapel (20)

With the Azabachería façade, this is the great work in the Cathedral of Archbishop Bartolomé Rajoy y Losada. It occupies the site of Archbishop Lope de Mendoza's (†1445) chapel of Our Lady of Pardon, where the graduation ceremonies of Santiago University used to take place.

Built like other Neo-classical buildings in Spain, it was planned by *Miguel Ferro Caaveiro*, in 1769. It was preceded by a narthex, which had two entrances, the one on the left, leading to the old chapel, having angels bearing the shield of the Mendozas, while the other, by *Tomás Gambino*, bore the arms of the Rajoys. In the vestibule one can still see the foundational inscription and the Gothic alabaster image of the Patron of the chapel, the Virgin of Pardon, a playfully disposed figure with the Child playing with a bird and His mother holding His bare foot, on a base showing the orant figure of the Archbishop. The piece has the features of international Gothic.

The chapel is a monumental rotunda where eight Ionic columns hold up a large dome and distribute the space with wide arches for the reredos and the mausoleums, while narrower ones cover a two-tier arrangement of lintelled doorways and niches above.

The reredos is by *Francisco de Lens*, and is dedicated to the Sacrament of Love, with the image of Sacred Heart, while the marble mausoleums, made in 1900 by *Ramón Constenla*, carved with images of Faith and Hope, give the chapel a symbolic unity.

The niches house four Doctors of the Church sculpted between 1603 and 1608 by *Juan da Vila* and *Gregorio Español*.

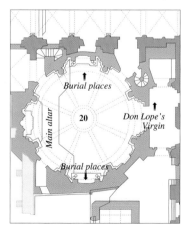

Virgin and Child in the old Chapel of Don Lope.

Right: *Detail of the Neo-classical chapel and its dome.*

Chapel of the Christ of Burgos (21)

This chapel was founded by Archbishop Pedro Carrillo and was built by the master craftsman from Santander *Melchor de Velasco y Agüero* between 1662 and 1664.

It is a noble proto-Baroque construction with a portal with double columns on dies and the founder's shield at the top. It has a Grecian groundplan and an architraved structure with great fluted pilasters supporting double coffered arches. The dome has pendentives bearing Carrillo's arms and ribs worked to form shells pouring water.

The main altarpiece is the fruit of the collaboration between *Bernardo Cabrera*, maker of Spain's first wreathed columns (on show in the museum) and *Mateo de Prado*, a disciple of Gregorio Fernández's. The crucifix was made in Burgos in the 18th Century, and replaces the original canvass. The side pieces of the "Tears of St Peter" and "The

Mother of the Zebedees", are of the school of *Mateo de Prado*.

Worthy of especial attention is the funerary niche of Pedro Carrillo, Archbishop and Captain General of Galicia (†1667), by *Pedro del Valle*, who wrought the kneeling figure with great craftsmanship and thorough naturist quality.

On the left is the tomb of Cardinal Miguel García (†1873), by the Compostelan sculptor *Cisneros*.

Left: *The Christ of Burgos.*

Praying figure of Don Pedro Carrillo

The Doors Leading down to the Crypt of the Portico of Glory (22)

From the last sections of the aisles, stairs lead down to the "lower church".

The portal of the south (right) aisle, which is also the entrance to the Chapel of the Relics (the old Chapter House), was part of the Renaissance work of the cloisters, according to plans made by *Juan de Alava* in the first third of the 16th Century.

The north portal, however, made in the mid 18th Century and attributed to *Simón Rodríguez*, is a spectacular composition bringing together Renaissance and Baroque elements of plates and scrolls with an unframed pediment where the corbels of the Romanesque impost surround a consecrational cross, topped out by scrolls, pinnacles and an angel holding a shell wrapped in acanthus leaves. This portal is an example of *Compostelan stylistic hybriding*, a mixing of the old and new, in which Simón was an expert.

Baroque doorway leading down to the Portico of Glory Crypt.

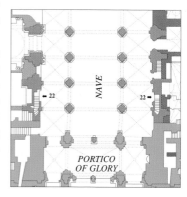

*O sol poniente, polas vidreiras
da soledade, lanza serenos
rayos, que firen descoloridos
da Gloria os anxeles y o Padre Eterno
Santos e apòstoles, ¡vedeos!, parece
cos labios moven, que falan quedo
os uns cos outros, e alò n'altura
do ceu a musica vai dar comenzo,
pois os groriosos concertadores
tempran riñosos os instrumentos.*

(Rosalía de Castro)

In 1168, King Ferdinand II granted Master Mateo a large annual pension to complete the Cathedral, a complex task which the lie of the land complicated yet more. The donation was exceptionally great and reveals the worth of an artist whose origins and education have been the object of diverse opinions, though his knowledge is recognized by all. He directed an active and important workshop.

COMPLETION OF THE NAVE AND AISLES:

The building of the nave and aisles went on for so long that they were not finished when Master Mateo took charge of the building. He respected their architectural organization, and only in the capitals of the last two pillars and in those of three sections of the triforium is the activity of his workshop to be noticed. Vegetable motifs predominate, although the representations of human forms and animals attract one's attention more.

THE PORTICO OF GLORY:

This is the western enclosing of the nave and aisles of the Cathedral, which brings together French, Italian and Hispanic influences. On the lintels of the tympanum it says that they were put in place by Master Mateo on the 1st April, 1188. Innovative ideas are introduced in its architecture, such as the pillars, unlike those of the rest of the building, pointed arches, ribbed vaulting and more illumination. The shape and subjects of the sculptures are also changed, as they are naturalist down to the smile and the dialogue. It is, then, a protogothic piece.

This wonderful ensemble was conceived and partly executed by Master Mateo. It is to him that such figures as the elderly musicians on the central arch are attributed, as are the Christ in the centre of the tympanum, St James on the mullion, the group made up of Moses, Isaiah, Daniel and Jeremiah, and one or two other pieces. But such a vast undertaking required several other master craftsmen whose names we do not know, and who have been studied by Professor Otero. One of them is distinguishable from the roughness of his pieces and the less fluid look of the garments, for example those of the evangelists, the angels on the tympanum, the groups of the blessed, the figures on the left-hand arch and the popular *Santo dos Croques* kneeling on the inside of the mullion. Other sculptors must have made the remaining statues, columns, figures on the inside of the Obradoiro façade, capitals, etc.

The tympanum, more comparable with French models than with Hispanic ones, has reliefs worked on slabs later set into it. Painting set off the ensemble, which has been the subject of repainting and retouching down the centuries.

Top: *Monsters on the plinths of the columns.*

Bottom and Right: *Plinth and mullion with Christ's genealogies: the human on the shaft, and the divine on the capital.*

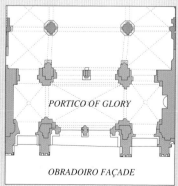

PORTICO OF GLORY

OBRADOIRO FAÇADE

Note: *Key to figures on the Portico inside back cover.*

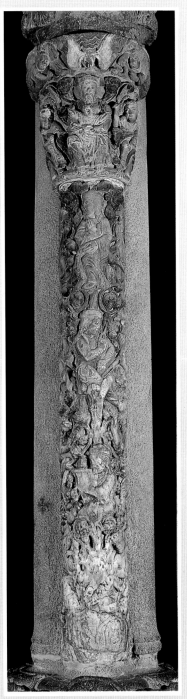

The pedestals are decorated with a fauna which includes a great number of fantastic creatures and fighting scenes. On the mullion a man opens the jaws of two lions, apparently representing Adam or Samson. In contrast with the wealth of detail on the pedestals, the shafts are plain, except those of marble, the one on the left of the central arch showing Isaac's sacrifice and the one opposite, the Resurrection. A third one, under the left-hand arch, is decorated not only with vegetable motifs but also with animals, centaurs and soldiers. The capitals and statue-columns are decorated with vegetable motifs or fighting animals and, like the

cymae, they follow typically Romanesque patterns.

Worthy of especial mention is the central column of the mullion, also of marble, on which is sculpted the Tree of Jesse. This human genealogy of Christ, among whose ancestors David and Mary may easily be distinguished, is completed with His divine genealogy in the Trinity on the capital, which in turn is the pedestal for the magnificent seated figure of St James. His pensive head bears a false halo of bronze and glass, like no other on the portico. In his right hand he is holding an inscription saying "The Lord sent me", while his right hand rests on a tau-shaped crozier. The capital of

the mullion narrates the temptations of Christ, with texts.

The statue columns portray prophets, apostles and other Old Testament personages who are not all recognizable as most of them lack signs of identity. The best known are those of the central arch, which are ideologically twinned: Moses with Peter (the heads of their respective churches), Isaiah with St Paul, Daniel with St James, and Jeremiah with John. The inspiration of the faces of the apostles in those of the prophets and the sculptural differences in the garments of the two groups are obvious.

The tympanum is presided by an impressive Christ showing His wounds. Behind His crowned and nimbused head

are angels with censers and He is flanked by the four evangelists and their respective signs. This apocalyptic vision is continued with the angels carrying the instruments of His Passion. Above them are choirs of the blessed. Seated in pairs around the arch are the Twenty-Four Elders with flasks of perfume and musical instruments, so accurately carved that reproductions of them have actually been used in concerts. Between the tympanum and the side arches angels help to send the saved through, thus endowing the ensemble with a conceptual unity. More angels and seraphim at

Prophets (left) and Apostles (right) on the Portico .

worship, situated on the inside, bring out the space of the portico.

The images on the archivolts on the left have given rise to different interpretations. On the greater arch, a fat bull imprisons some people with long streamers without inscriptions. They represent ten of the tribes of Israel shackled by the laws of Moses, while the other two, together with Adam, Eve and various Biblical personages are to be found between the leaves of the inner archivolt, which is presided over by Christ and shows His descent into Limbo. This sort of Judgement of God's Chosen People is somehow completed by the one on the archivolts on the right. On the keystones are the heads of Christ and St Michael, on their right, the blessed, taken by angels to glory, and on their left, the reprobate, tortured by serpents and extravagant demons according to their vices and sins. Four angels with trumpets occupy the corners.

The apocalyptic vision of the Portico of Glory cumulates in the gallery, which is higher than the roof of the Cathedral. On the keystone of its vault is an Agnus Dei, the lamp which illuminates the

celestial Jerusalem. The ribs spring from thurifying angels, and rose windows were made on each side, the western one being lost when the Obradoiro façade was built. The light it admitted used to reach the nave through the circular window and quatrefoil openings over the arches of the triforium.

The Portico of Glory was completed by an outer façade, known from old drawings, remains and research. In the construction of the Obradoiro, which replaced it, the architectural solutions supporting the vaults were retained, which explains the survival of certain figures on the inside of the portico. Others, from the demolished parts, are in museums and private collections, and two are on the railings of the Obradoiro. Remains of arches and other elements are to be found in the Cathedral Museum. The twin square towers standing at the sides of the façade were used as the bases of the present towers.

Left: *Detail of the tympanum; angels bearing the Cross.*

Tympanum with an apocalyptic vision and a seated figure of the Apostle St James on the mullion.

The Treasury Anteroom (23)

A 17th-Century door gives access to a number of rooms set around Alava's new cloisters.

In the vestibule, with low ribbed vaults is kept the tombstone of Theudemirus, the finder of the Apostle's tomb in the 9th Century: "In this grave lies God's servant Theudemirus, bishop of Iria Flavia, who died on the XIII kalendes of November in the year DCCCLXXXV of our era" (20th October, 847).

Two 19th Century paintings by *Juan José Cancela*, the "Ecce Homo" and the "Dolorosa", belong to the retrochoir of the Cathedral choir. There are two commemorative inscriptions: one of Pope John XXIII's stay in Santiago and one concerning Thomas Valois, bishop of Cashel, Ireland, who was banished in 1654. There is also a canvass of St Felix of Cantalicio, from the school of Murillo.

Reredos-Cathedral Reliquary, in the Chapel of the Relics.

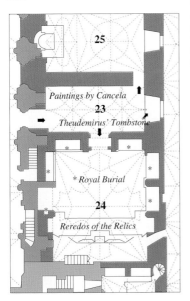

Chapel of the Relics and Royal Burial Vault (24)

A door with an arch of mixed lines, typical of Salamanca, leads to a high room with a beautiful openwork vault in the style of the late Gothic of Burgos, with ogee ribs springing from corbels.

The present reredos, made of Cuban cedar, donated by Galician emigrants, was designed by *Rafael de la Torre* and executed by *Maximino Magariños* in 1924. It replaced *Bernardo Cabrera* and *Gregorio Español's* Mannerist altarpiece of 1630, burnt down on the 2nd May, 1921, of which important remains are preserved: the Virtues of Fortitude and Temperance, in their original niches, and, in the Museum, the first wreathed columns made in Spain and boards showing the life of the Apostle and Virtues.

The Royal Burial Vault. The medieval royal sarcophagi were brought to this setting of 17th Century architecture from their original resting place in 1535. The history of the Compostelan burial vault is connected with the building of the Romanesque basilica. It contains a beautiful collection of gravestones, presided over by that of Ferdinand II (†1188), who was a patron of Master Mateo and his works. The king's recumbent effigy is from his workshop, and is novel in portraying him peacefully asleep, which set a pattern for the other two - Gothic - tombs of men: those of Alfonso IX (†1230), promoter of the Cathedral's consecration of 1211, and Raymond of Burgundy (†1107). The statue of Doña Berenguela (†1149), the beautiful wife of Alfonso VII, also dates from the beginning of the 13th Century.

The sarcophagus of Doña Juana de Castro, the wife of Peter I, the Just, belongs to the last third of the 14th Century.

They are accompanied by the Count of Traba, Don Pedro Froilaz, in a sarcophagus of the 12th Century, the reclining form on which was made by *Maximino Magariños* in 1926, following historicist artistic trends.

The Compostelan collection comprises first-class reliquaries and relics. A list follows of the some pieces of great historical and devotional value: *Cross of the scrolls* (11th Cent.); The *Apostle's Cross* (also called Ordoño II's cross) (11th Cent.), *Carboeiro Cross*, or cross of the Patriarchate of Jerusalem (12th Cent.), *St James Coquatriz*, Parisian workshop (13th-14th Cent.), *Caput Argenteum*, the reliquary of the Head of St James

Alphaeus, of beaten silver, gilded and enamelled, with classical precious stones, cameos and intaglios, made at a Compostelan workshop in 1322; *Don Lope de Mendoza's Compostelan Collection* (15th Cent.); Reliquary of *St Pauline* by *Jorge Cedeira* "O Vello" (The Elder) 16th Cent.

There are *enamels*, such as the cover of the 12th-Century *Gospel Book*, 13th-Century ivories of the *Virgin and Child* and 15th-Century jet pieces of *St Clare*.

Top: *Statue-reliquary of St Theresa de Jesús and ivory figure of Christ (17th Century).*

Bottom: *Recumbent sculpture of Ferdinand II.*

Right: *Vault with openwork cells and a bust-reliquary of St James Alphaeus.*

The Treasury (25)

It is what used to be the medieval Treasury from the 9th Century to the 16th. Since the 17th Century it has been a chapel dedicated to St Ferdinand. It has a rectangular groundplan, with ribbed vaults on corbels, divided by an arch which leads to a nave, and a back wall with a niche.

The lunettes show murals painted in 1536 by Pedro Noble of the *Ascension* and the *Assumption*.

The small Renaissance altarpiece with a reliquary is by *Cornielis of Holland*.

There are important collections of sacred vessels, crosses, trays and other objects representative of the history of gold- and silversmithing.

Worthy of especial mention are *Antonio de Arfe's Processional Taberna-* cle, *Juan Posse's* late 17th-Century ciborium, *Juan de Figueroa's* early 18th-Century tabernacle and *Archbishop Múzquiz's Chalice*, made in Madrid by *Lucas de Foro* in the 19th Century.

Left: *Antonio de Arfe's processional tabernacle.*

Treasury Vault

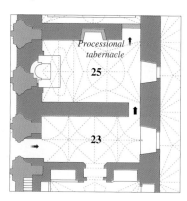

The Organs (26)

The organs take up the last sections of the nave and endow it with a sumptuous character. Their conception and ornamentation links them with *Andrade*, and they were built between 1705 and 1713 by *Miguel de Romay* and *Antonio Alfonsín*. They indicate the site of the Cathedral choir area, first occupied by Master Mateo's stone choir, made in Gelmírez's time, and then, from the end of the 16th Century until their dismantling in 1945, by the wooden stalls made by *Juan da Vila* and *Gregorio Español*, (now preserved at *Sobrado de los Monjes, Coruña*).

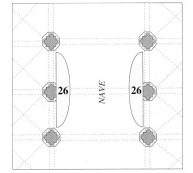

Preceding double page:

Left: *Cup from the donation of the Duke and Duchess of Montpensier. Silver scallop shell.*

Right: *Mexican altar cruet set. English polychromed alabaster Pax Brede.*

The Crossing

The crossing, the intersection of the nave and the transept, is crowned by the *tambour*. Robust pillars support the four arches, which, together with squinches, take us up to the octagonal dome. Trumpeting angels and the armorial bearings of Don Lope de Mendoza indicate the transition from the Romanesque to the Gothic, in which style the tambour is built, probably to replace a Romanesque one. It was begun in 1384 and is by *Sancho Martís*.

The columns at the angles of the octagon become elongated ribs, which meet at the central keystone for the tambour to be covered with eight deep cells. From a height of thirty-two metres, its great windows bathe the whole basilica in light, bringing out the classic beauty of its architecture.

Baroque alterations changed the windows and added the balustrade, supported by atlantes.

Left: *Baroque organs.*

Central section of the transept with the tambour.

The *Botafumeiro* (The Great Censer)

The Botafumeiro was first mentioned in 1322, in connection with the reliquary of the head of St James Alphaeus, which is brought out in diocesan processions, according to a note in the margin of the *Calixtine Codex*. The Medieval system of swinging the great censer in the arms of the transept was replaced in the 16th Century by the present device, planned by the Aragonese artist *Juan Bautista Celma* and made at the *Herrerías de Vizcaya* (Biscay Smithies), whereby a spool, spinning in alternate directions, is mounted on two intersecting arches. The *Turibulum magnum*, or "king of censers", is swung by eight *tiraboleiros* pulling a thick rope. The botafumeiro is normally kept in the Cathedral museum, and the *artichoke* (a model) is hung in its place.

The Reliquary of St James's Staff (27)

On the southern pillar of the crossing is a bronze column 228 centimetres high made at the end of the 12th Century. It has a spiral shaft formed by plain bands and a wide strip edged with pearls and decorated with scrolls, linked with the columns of the Portico of Glory.

It may have been the stem of a ciborium, used to house the staff which tradition considers to be St James's, together with the stick of St Franco of Senna, who in the 13th Century recovered his eyesight on a pilgrimage to Compostela. The statue of the Pilgrim Apostle crowning it is 16th Century. It used to be visited by pilgrims.

Left: *Botafumeiro swung by the* tiraboleiros *to reach the vaults of the transept.*

One of the richly decorated pulpits.

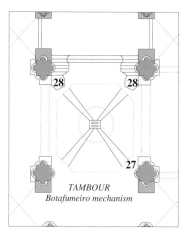

TAMBOUR
Botafumeiro mechanism

The Pulpits (28)

Each of these bronze pieces made by *Juan Bautista Celma* in 1578, situated on either side of the chancel, is formed by a high pedestal with three atlantes supporting sirens holding the base. The balustrade with telamones has a frieze with apostles and prophets flanking Jacobean scenes. The left-hand pulpit bears reproductions of the reliefs on Antonio de Arfe's tabernacle (in the Cathedral museum), while the right-hand one has original reliefs by Celma concerning the *Battle of Clavijo* and the *Tribute of the Hundred Maidens*.

The testers are by *Miguel de Romay* (1714).

The Alms Boxes (29)

These are on the pillars of the chancel, with seated figures of polychromed granite. On the left is the image of *St James Alphaeus*, made in 1393, with strong reminiscences of Master Mateo's school. The inscription reads: "*Ecce arca Hóperis Beati Iacobi Apóstoli*", with medieval reminders concerning the alms box for Cathedral works. On the right is *St Mary Salome*, Zebedee's wife and the mother of James and John, carved in the 16th Century, like the alms boxes themselves.

St James Alphaeus and St Mary Salome, polychromed stone petitionary figures

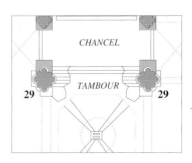

The Chancel

It is here that the basilica is to be seen at its best.The Romanesque construction is conserved, although far-reaching changes have been made in ornamentation.

The split-level arrangement is caused by the presence of the apostolic mausoleum under the whole upper part of the chancel floor beyond the lower flight of steps. The mausoleum used to be as high as the baldachin is today, but was destroyed by Archbishop Gelmírez in 1106 and replaced by the Romanesque platal: ciborium, altar and small altarpiece over the tomb, which lasted until the present Baroque work was constructed in the second half of the 17th Century.

The Romanesque architectural harmony is formed by two tiers of arcades opening onto the ambulatory and the gallery. Of openwork construction, it allowed the passage of light. Pilgrims used to be able to visit the tomb and keep vigil from the ambulatory. Hidden at the back of the semicircular retrochoir is Gelmírez's old *confessio*, where the floor level is lower beyond the top of the mausoleum.

To the Romanesque Cathedral new constructions were continually added, to break the unitarian aspect of its architecture, the charm of which had been spoilt. Even the modern period was not lacking in an efficient man to carry out a far-reaching programme of alterations in line with contemporary trends: the famous Canon Vega y Verdugo, who introduced the Baroque style to Compostela, where it acquired certain airs of originality. Together with his *Report*, which includes his thoughts concerning the Basilica of St James, the sponsor forms the school that will see his pro-gramme developed and carried out, between 1657 and 1751, giving rise to an *architecture within an architecture* and to *stylistic hybriding*, grafting the new onto the old and moulding the new into the old, a point of view which is important for understanding the Cathedral. The chancel, the Chapter's main preoccupation, was intentionally included in the Cathedral alterations. To the church's *raison d'être*, the apostle's tomb and the traditional pilgrimages with their jubilee years, are added the revitalizing of the national heritage concerning St James the Great and the prestige of the tomb, to which are also added the economic supremacy and patronage of the archbishops, giving rise to the spread of the Baroque, which the pilgrim may contemplate in its most spectacular form.

Vega y Verdugo completely emptied the chancel,conferring on it a completely new aspect, and lowered yet further the height of the mausoleum to leave it as it is today.

The *Camarín*, alone in the middle of the chancel, crowns the Tomb over which it is built as an indication of its presence. It is made up of a great pedestal of jaspers, the *Bocelón*, hollowed out to contain a beautiful stone, the *Cenotaph*, where there used to be an altar with an arcaded front, so that the *Camarín* might be seen from the basilica, though today it is hidden by the silver altar front, and only visible from the ambulatory.

From the ambulatory, one enters the *Templete* (pavilion), where one can see the venerable seated image from Master Mateo's workshop, which has presided over the basilica since its consecration in 1211. Re-dressed as a pilgrim since the 16th Century, the image holds a tablet saying *"Hic est corpus dici Iacobi Apos-*

toli et Hispaniarum Patroni". The lamp was donated by the Great Captain in 1512. In front of the image are the four votive lamps of Alfonso XI, in memory of the Battle of Salado (1340).

The Camarín is crowned by the figure of the Pilgrim Apostle, surrounded by Kings Alfonso II, Ramiro II, Ferdinand II and Philip IV, bringing out the royal patronage. They are by *Pedro del Valle*, as is the retable at the back of the

Camarín, with illustrations depicting the life of St James.

At the end of the 17th Century, owing to Archbishop Monroy's generosity, the Camarín was enriched with the Baroque silverwork designed by the master craftsman *Friar Gabriel de las Casas* and executed by the Salamanca silversmith *Juan de Figueroa* in 1700.

Chancel with Baroque baldachin (left). Detail: stone figure of St James.

Filigreed pilasters with plates, angels and vegetable motifs flank the pavilion, where the apostle sits on a silver throne, with his pilgrim's cloak and staff. The ensemble is finished off by the extraordinary Glory medallion, with God the Father amid nimbi, born by seraphim and worshipped by cherubim.

On the altar is the splendid ensemble of the tabernacle and display cabinet with solomonic pilasters with eucharistic vines. It is accompanied by statuettes of St Peter and St Paul, the Doctors of the Church and allegories of Faith and Hope. Inside it is the image of the Immaculate Virgin, the fruit of the collaboration between the sculptor *Manuel de Prado y Mariño* and the silversmith *Jabcobo Pecul*. The front part is by the Compostelan *Antonio de Montaos*. The Rococo gates made in 1765 by *Angel Piedra* complete the piece. The main lamp and chandelier are by the French silversmith *Louis Baladier*, and were donated by the Cathedral schoolmaster Diego Juan de Ulloa.

The amazing *baldachin* was designed by *Antonio de Andrade*, who used ideas and drawings by Vega y Verdugo. Eight angels bear the great canopy of three graceful tiers, full of symbols of the Apostle's patronage. The first tier includes the royal arms, accompanied by the cardinal virtues, and the second one shows the apparition of St James at Clavijo. By *Mateo de Prado*, the whole is topped out with the ark and star born by angels, symbolizing the glorification of the Tomb, against the blue background of the vaults.

The decoration is completed with the covering of the pillars and columns of the chapel with solomonic columns on jasper pedestals.

Top: *Image of the Apostle's "Embrace".*

Bottom: *Steps to the Apostle's Camarín.*

Following Page:

Baptismal Font (left). *Clavijo tympanum* (right).

THE PLATERIAS ARM OF THE TRANSEPT

In the Platerías arm, with a new view of the halls of the transept, we conclude our tour of the basilica.

J. Beltrán de Guevara's Tomb (30)

In the arm's eastern aisle is the mausoleum of Archbishop Juan Beltrán de Guevara (†1622), designed by *Bartolomé Fernández Lechuga*.

In the floor is a grille giving access down to the excavations, with remains of Roman constructions and of Alfonso III's basilica.

Doorway leading to the Royal Door on Quintana Square (31)

It is on the site of the Romanesque apse dedicated to St John the Baptist and was planned by *Antonio de Andrade* in 1657.

Baptismal Font (32)

A conjunction of Romanesque structures forms the hidden corner where the pre-Romanesque 9th-Century *baptismal font* is kept, from which Almanzor's horse drank during the raid in 997.

In the opposite corner is the entrance to the vestment wardrobe (Baroque doorway).

Martín López's Tomb (33)

Against the wall is the sepulchre of Canon Cardinal Martín López (†1477), with a late Gothic recumbent statue.

The Clavijo Tympanum (33)

Set into the wall is the composition known as the *Clavijo Tympanum*, which must have been brought here from the Gothic cloister in the 13th Century. The archivolt bears angels in an arcade, inspired by models by Master Mateo. On the tympanum, St James is depicted on horseback with a sword and flag, with the inscription: *Sancti Iacobi, Apóstolus Christi*, and surrounded by feminine figures in allusion to the *Tribute of a Hundred Maidens*.

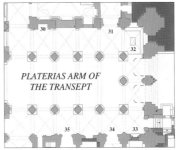

PLATERIAS ARM OF THE TRANSEPT

THE CLOISTER AND ITS DOORWAYS

The beautiful 13th-Century cloister had been ruined bythe bellicose impact of the Galician nobility, the local bourgeoisie and the Archbishops of Santiago throughout the Middle Ages, which, together with the shortage of space, made it advisable to build a new one. The decision was taken by the Archbishop and sponsor Alonso de Fonseca III. Work was begun in 1521 and was not finished until 1590. The plan was by *Juan de Alava*, who directed works until his death in 1537, thus forging a link between Santiago and Valladolid. The work was continued by *Rodrigo Gil de Hontañón*.

It is one of the best cloisters in Spain, having spacious loggias 34 metres long and 6 metres wide with other departments off them: to the north, the sacristy and anteroom, the treasury, the Chapel of the Relics and the Dawn (Alba) Chapel; to the east, the cloister vestibule, All Souls Chapel, Canons' vestry and, upstairs, the galleries and wardrobe, with its tower. In the southeast corner is the Records Tower.

The cloister and its decoration have a symbolism which make it one unit, dedicated to the Virgin Mary. The building itself is, as it were, a *Hortus Conclusus*, or *Closed Garden*, in allusion to Virginity.

On the outer wall, the Treasury Façade, the upper row of medallions shows the genealogy of Jesus, according to the Gospel of St Matthew, presided over by the medallion of the Virgin and Child to the right. The tower bearing the medallions of the leaders of Israel is the *Tower of David*, of Marian significance.

The Entrances to the Cloister and Sacristy (34-35)

These form part of the plan of the cloister as accesses from the basilica, and are essential pieces in the interpretation of its iconography.

The two beautiful doorways, identically built, fit the vertical spaces of the Romanesque sections. The balanced arrangement of their rectangular spaces in a perfect geometric pattern forms a triumphal arch on each door. They are *Retable Doorways* in the strictest Plateresque taste, with beautiful sculpture decoration by *Maestre Arnao*, a collaborator of *Juan de Alava's*.

All this symbolism leads us into the cloister, the doorway to which bears the scenes of the *Annunciation* and *Incarnation of the Son of God*. From the pediment the Eternal Father blesses human Redemption, and all the sculptures are linked with this representation: the protecting griffins, the eagles of the Resurrection and the snakes and dolphins, respectively the symbols of sin and salvation, resolved in the pains of the Virgin, Mother of Beautiful Love.

The medallions portray Archbishops Fonseca II and III.

The sacristy doorway has a secondary iconography connected with the access to the Chapel of the Relics and

Detail of the arcades of the cloister and the Plateresque frieze.

Following double page:

Renaissance doorways: cloister (left) *and sacristy* (right).

the Treasury. The left-hand niche contains St James the Apostle and Pilgrim. He is accompanied by St Ildefonso, patron saint of the funder, Alonso de Fonseca III. In the spandrels of the doors we can see the representation of Valour, in reference to St James, and Wisdom, in reference to the saint from Toledo, and also to Fonseca, who was renowned for his culture. In the pediment is St James, the Protector, in Glory.

The symbols of the façade bear a relationship with those of the Platerías Façade, portraying St James, his miracles and emblems, with the discoverers of the Tomb and the bishops who built the cloister.

The Picture of the Apostle is by *Juan Antonio García de Bouzas*.

The *high-vaulted sacristy* contains a collection of Flemish pictures of the 18th Century, Baroque painting of the 17th Century and 19th Century neoclassical art.

The Plateresque Cloister

The Gothic profiles of its architecture are brought together with Renaissance ornamentation. The loggias are made up of five sections, each of which has an exterior buttress with diversely shaped pinnacles and is finished off with a cornice and openwork cresting. Inside, sheaves of ribs spring from the high corbels to form the stellate vaults, which are constructed with a variety of keystones. An interesting frieze, as if made by a silversmith, goes round the whole cloister, like a bracelet. Its subjects complete the symbolism, alluding to the triumph of Resurrection over Death, thus stressing the cemeterial nature of the place.

Indeed, it is a cemetery of canons, where such renowned churchmen as Amor Ruibal and López Ferreiro are laid to rest, and where there is a large collection of heraldry of the Galician nobility.

The collection of monumental brasses includes those of Archbishops of the 17th and 18th Centuries, and there are sarcophagi of canons from the 14th century to the 16th.

The bells, taken from the Clock Tower, are 18th Century and were replaced with new ones in 1989.

In the courtyard is the *Fons Mirabilis*, which Gelmírez had built around 1122 and which Aymerico Picaud described in the *Calixtine Codex* and saw it installed in the atrium of Paradise.

North side (bottom) and East side (right) of the cloister.

The *Alba* (Dawn) Chapel (36)

Founded in 1529 by Canon Gómez Ballo, it is the Rivero de Aguilar family vault.

The splendid 18th-Century altarpiece of the Transfiguration of Christ may be

Tumbo A: miniature of Ferdinand III, the Saint.

Left: Neo-Classical reredos of the Transfiguration in the Dawn (Alba) Chapel.

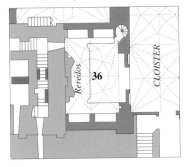

attributed to the workshop of *José Gambino*. Use was made of an earlier one with the Tabor scene with St Peter, St James and St John, linked with the 17th-Century artist *Mateo de Prado*.

The Cathedral Archives

In the south-west corner is the door to the Chapter Archives, whose rooms are covered with Baroque plate vaults built by *Lucas Ferro Caaveiro* in the 18th Century.

A wealth of documents are kept here, noteworthy among which are the Calixtine Codex, or Liber Sancti Iacobi, written by Aymerico Picaud around 1139; the *Historia Compostelana*, which tells us about the deeds of Archbishop Diego Gelmírez; and *Tumbo A*, begun about 1129.

THE OBRADOIRO ROOMS

At the beginning of the 17th Century, when the cloister was finished, new buildings were built onto its south and west loggias, sponsored by Archbishop Juan de Sanclemente y Torquemada and planned by *Jácome Fernández*, to form the Obradoiro cloister façade.

A door with Sanclemente y Torquemada's arms leads to the Library, Chapter House and Museums. After the first two were destroyed by fire, they were rebuilt by *Lucas Ferro Caaveiro* in 1751, with flattened granite vaults.

The Chapter Library (37)

The vault is made up of a large central flat ceiling supported by segments of arches, between which there are lunettes over the cornice, which are decorated with Jacobean symbols. The frescoes and sanguines of the Apostle's life were painted by *Arias Varela* in 1756.

The bookshelves house many notable collections and incunabula.

The choir lectern is by *Juan da Vila* and *Gregorio Español* (17th Century).

The examination pulpit (where aspirant canons were examined –*translator's note*) was made by *Francisco de Lens* in the 18th Century.

The *botafumeiro* (censer) was made in 1851 by *José Losada* and its replica, in silver, was donated to the Apostle-Saint by the Provisional Second Lieutenants of the Spanish Armed Forces.

The Chapterhouse (38)

It is covered with a flattened vault and is surprising because of the technical mastery and beautiful decoration of the extensive carving in hard granite. It was whitewashed and painted by *Tomás Aguiar*.

The room is presided over by the altar, with a frontal by the Italian *Sernini* and the image of St James as a pilgrim made in 1754 by *José Gambino*. At the sides are oils on copper by *Juan Antonio García de Bouzas*, with scenes of the "Road to Calvary" and the "Battle of Puente Milvio".

At the opposite end is the top table, a Rococo design by *Ferro Caaveiro*, with a canopy which is an imitation of the models by Guillermo Anglois made at the Royal Factory of St Barbara in 1764 for Charles III's bedroom. The painting of the "Apparitions of the Virgin of Guadeloupe" was painted by the Mexican artist *Juan Patricio Morlete* in 1769. On the left is a tapestry of the Neapolitan series, donated by Philip IV in 1665.

There is a magnificent collection of 16th-Century Flemish tapestries illustrating the life of Scipio.

Also to be seen are 18th-Century ballot boxes in mother of pearl and ivory and a 17th Century footwarmer with symbols relating to St James.

Flattened granite vaults decorated with paintings and reliefs in the Library (top) and Chapter House (bottom).

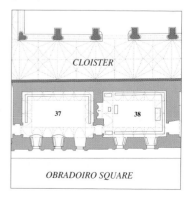

MUSEUM

The Obradoiro Rooms

Room I houses the results of *archeological digs* made in 1878-79 and from 1940 to 1960 in the apostolic mausoleum and the Cathedral subsoil, concerning the 1st-11th Centuries.

There is a collection of Roman *milestones* and *altars of the* 1st-4th Centuries.

Early Christian pieces from Galicia include the *Setecoros capitals and the Caracacia plaques* (4th-6th Centuries).

Ninth-Century archeological pieces of the pre-Romanesque *Compostelan basilicas* of Alfonso II and Alfonso III are on show.

Room II shows the Romanesque basilica and Pilgrim art in a museum setting, with pieces and plans: *St James's church and the phases of construction*: 1, the first phase, Master Bernardo the Elder and his workshop, 1075-1088; and 2, the second phase, 1093-1140, *Master Esteban* and his workshop, with a set of interesting pieces such as the marble columns of Paradise, the "Admonishing of Adam and Eve", the "Month of February" and "Christ in Majesty".

The *Bucheria**

Room I displays the last phase of the building of the Romanesque Cathedral: *Master Mateo* and his workshop, 1160-1211, with: 1, reconstructions of the west face (arches, rose windows, imposts and sculptures) and 2, the stone choir, with a reconstruction of one of its sections with four seats, and other structures from it.

Room II houses reconstructions of the beautiful medieval cloister.

Room III exhibits the singular chapter of Gothic sculpture, from the 13th to the 16th Centuries, including the "Goodyear" reredos and the "Annunciation" group (15th Century) and the "Three Generations" (16th Century).

Room IV contains wood carvings from the 13th Century to the 18th, with pieces by *Juan Bautista Celma, Gregorio Español, Juan de Vila* and *Bernardo Cabrera*, as well as 17th- and 18th-Century paintings.

* From French *boucheries* (butcher's), butcher's shops having existed here –*translator's note.*

Niche with an angel.

Right: *Rose window from the original front* (top) *and fragment from the reconstruction of the cresting of the stone choir* (bottom).

Preceding double page:

Left: *Virgin of the Annunciation in polychromed stone.*

Right, from top to bottom: *Goodyear reredos. The Moving of the Apostle's Body. St Anne, the Virgin and Child. Mudéjar decoration.*

Stone tympanum showing the entry into Jerusalem (top) and St Joseph's Dream, in wood (bottom).

Right: Top, *Gothic Annunciation in stone* and, bottom, *St Joseph's dream, in wood.*

The Gallery Rooms

These are situated on the lst floor of the Obradoiro façade, and open onto the covered gallery on Obradoiro Square, with views of the city.

Room I contains a collection of tapestries by *Ginés de Aguirre, A. del Castillo* and *Teniers*, together with solomonic columns and Virtues by *Gregorio Español* and *Bernardo Cabrera* (17th Century).

There is also the pennant from the flagship of the Battle of Lepanto, donated to the Apostle by John of Austria in 1571.

Room II houses a collection of tapestries by *Rubens* and his disciple *Van Thulden*, with episodes from the life of Achilles, from the *Juan Raës* factory (Brussels, 1528).

Room III has a collection by *Teniers* of country topics with scenes of every-day life and fiestas (Royal Tapestry Factory, Madrid, 18th Century), and blue tapestries: "The Game of Skittles" and "The Slaughtering of the Pig" from Juan de Melter's workshop, Lille, France.

Room IV contains tapestries by *A. González Ruíz* and *Francisco Bayeu* from the Royal Tapestry Factory, Madrid (18th Century).

Room V displays tapestries based on cartoons by *Francisco Goya*, Royal Factory, 1776-1808.

There are also pictures by the 18th-Century Compostelan painter *Gregorio Ferro*, who was Director of the Royal Academy of Painting of St Ferdinand, Madrid.

Bottom: *The Holy Family and the Supper, by José del Castillo.*

Right: *The Blind Guitarrist, by Goya.*

Following double page: *The Goddess Pan, by Rubens.*Following page: *Safeguarding the Tobacco, by Goya.*